The Old
Zen Master

Inspirations
for Awakening

Trevor Leggett

Buddhist Publishing Group

Totnes, England

Buddhist Publishing Group
Sharpham Coach Yard
Ashprington
Totnes, TQ9 7UT

Edited by Diana St Ruth

British Library Catalogue in Publication data
A Catalogue record for this book is available from
the British Library

ISBN 0-946672-29-6

Printed in the UK by Cromwell Press on acid free paper.

To the late

Dr Hari Prasad Shastri

who introduced me to Zen in its original Indian form,
in whom the ancient traditions were always young,
these pieces are reverently dedicated by this pupil.

Contents

Foreword

In this rather freewheeling book—and it has to be freewheeling—I am trying to give a few hints which have helped me and which can be of help to others. It is like pepper and salt with a meal. They are not the nourishment itself, but sometimes they can make the nourishment easier to take and digest. You cannot live on pepper and salt! So nothing replaces the solid practice, study and devotion of the life. Occasionally, however, a new slant, a new angle, or a new illustration—especially if it is an unexpected one—can be a help in absorbing some of these things.

However, some of these stories contain a germ of life of their own which if discovered and meditated upon can produce a spurt of inner growth. My teacher said that if a phrase particularly strikes, it should be memorized and gone into more deeply in the subsequent weeks to find the hidden meaning. Some of the sayings of Bukko in this book would be ideal for the purpose.

What I say comes from various sources—from teachers I have heard, from things I have read, I take temple magazines, and occasionally people write a little memoir of their own teachers which contain very useful pointers.

Truth

We are told in the holy texts of Buddhism, as well as in other traditions, to speak the truth. And what we say should be beneficial, should be pleasantly uttered, and should not cause excitement. When I speak, I can decide whether to tell the truth, say something that simply doesn't matter, or perhaps just utter vicious lies. It is my decision. As a matter of fact, I often decide to tell the truth, but there is something quite different from this. If I speak the truth, I am a good man while I am speaking it, but there is something higher than goodness.

The Brahmins of India were not supposed to have executive power. They were to be men of piety and learning who taught the holy texts, and morality when it was needed. They would get a fee for this. They could even reprimand kings, but must speak the truth. The following is a traditional case that was told to me.

There was a famine. One of the local farmers had foreseen the coming calamity and had cornered the local rice market. He had bought the rice cheap and it was piled high in his granary which stood next to his house. As the shortage of rice began to be felt, he was able to raise the price and raise the price and raise the price. The poor were starving but the rich were willing to pay the high prices.

One day the poor met. Among them was a poor Brahmin who was also starving. The carpenter said that there was a weak place in the granary which stood next to the rich farmer's house. He could make a hole in it large enough for a man to wriggle through, who could then pass out the rice in a bowl to the poor outside. And this they agreed to do.

The Brahmin said that he should be the one to do it. Burglary and theft were punishable by death in that kingdom, but he said, 'As I am a Brahmin, they will not kill me. I shall be disgraced, humiliated publicly, and exiled. But they will not kill me.'

All went well. In the middle of the night the Brahmin got through the hole successfully, stood inside the granary and ladled out the rice with a bowl into the little sacks of the poor.

Meanwhile, next door to the granary, the owner was looking over his books and congratulating himself on making a real killing. 'I can hang on for another three weeks and I'll squeeze the last penny out of the rich,' he gloated, 'The poor will get by, somehow, and then I will be able to extend my holdings and become one of the most influential men of the district.'

And then, to his amazement, a voice boomed from the granary, 'O deluded man, these things are merely passing. Repent! Devote your talents to serving your fellow men, not exploiting them.'

The owner at once called the strong-arm watchman and together they dashed into the granary and arrested the Brahmin.

Next morning they brought him before the magistrate. But the magistrate praised the Brahmin and said, 'You have performed your duty as a Brahmin by speaking the truth and giving moral instruction where it was clearly needed. As your fee for the spiritual instruction which you gave, I order that half the remaining rice in the granary shall be made over to you to be disposed of as you wish.'

Then he stood up and made a reverence to the Brahmin and said, 'May I do my duty as a magistrate with the same fearlessness as you have done yours as a Brahmin.'

This is the traditional story. A good person speaks the truth, but there comes a time when the truth speaks through a good person regardless of any circumstances or any consequences, and this story illustrates that. When some of the silt in the channel has been removed, then it is Truth declaring the truth, not a person declaring the truth.

Perfection

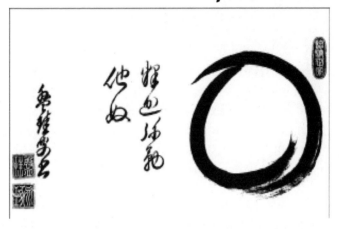

Zen calligraphy often brushes a circle to represent Perfection. It is sometimes a massive ring, but in this piece by Bankei the circle is merely hinted at with two light strokes.

The poem reads in free translation:

> *Not the Buddha of the past,*
> *Nor the Buddha of the future—*
> *This is someone else.*

The poem refers to a phrase in the Mumonkan classic, which refers to some fellow who is not (the classical Buddha) Shakyamuni nor Maitreya (the Buddha to come).

The calligrapher is the famous seventeenth-century Japanese Zen priest Bankei. who spread what he termed 'Unborn Zen', corresponding to the Indian doctrine of A-jata-vada, the teaching that nothing has ever been born.

Forty

This is from my personal experience as a judo man. Although it is technical, the technical point itself is of no importance to the story which, perhaps, can help you. I know that it works.

I will just sketch out the judo position. When you meet the opponent you can get a hold on the lapel with one hand on the inside, and you have to be content with the other hand holding the other lapel on the outside. This is because opponents do not face each other quite directly. It would be an advantage to have both hands inside, but your opponent won't let you do that.

Now, you may meet another opponent who insists on putting his second hand inside as well, which would give an advantage. It is quite easy to throw the second hand off, and you do it immediately. Then he comes and puts it in again, and you throw it off again. Generally, opponents will accept that, but this opponent does it again . . . and you throw him off . . . and he does it again . . . and you throw him off . . . and he does it again . . .

Then you lose your temper. You make a big movement: *GET OUT . . !* That's when he throws you!

Your big angry response has weakened your posture. He cannot maintain his second hand inside, but he keeps bringing it in. You go on throwing it off until you lose your temper, thinking, 'Oh, for God's sake, why do I always seem to end up practising with idiots?'

Alternatively, when your opponent keeps doing this, you may get fed up and just think, 'Oh well, let him have it.' Then he has an advantage.

Now, what do you do? It is so idiotic. Either you lose your temper, or you put up with it. The answer is in one word—*forty*. He comes in and you throw him off—*one*. He comes in and you throw him off—*two*. He comes in and you throw him off—*three*. You are prepared to go on for forty times without losing your temper.

When he finds, after six or seven times, that you have not lost your temper nor become disconcerted, he gets tired. Then he stops doing it.

How can this be applied in other ways? We get some persistent thought which we know is pretty idiotic, but it persists: 'They said *this* about me! They keep saying *this!*' And you throw it off. Then the thought comes back: 'They're forming little groups and running me down!' The thoughts keep coming back, mindlessly. The thought, the impulse to do something, the sexual impulse, the ambitious impulse, keeps on mindlessly coming back.

Instead of putting it away a few times and then losing your temper and getting angry with it, or saying, 'Oh, I'll never get rid of this', remember 'forty times'. The thought comes, no!—*one*; you get on with what you are doing. It comes again, no!—*two*; you get on with what you are doing. The thought comes again, no!—*three*; you get on with what you are doing. After a few more times, it gets tired! We think it won't, but it gets tired, because it lives on our reactions; it is powered by our reactions.

So, when you are lying in bed with some persistent worry be prepared to count up to forty, putting that worry aside. *It* doesn't count up to forty, it isn't very bright and it doesn't know how long you will resist.

In connection with this, there is a point to make on *shila*, morality. Oka Kyugaku said that moral behaviour—to be reasonable about things, to be honest, to be self-restrained, and so on—seems to be unnatural and forced. 'I want something but I must not take it.' That seems to be unnatural.

Oka said that this is because we have acquired unnatural attitudes. We can compare it to teaching a child to write. Children naturally hold a pen low down near the nib which cramps their writing. But later on they ought to be told to hold the pen higher up and loosen their grip which is how 160 words per minute expert shorthand writers hold their pens. They don't have to keep moving their hands across the page with every word as the children do. When one is made to sit up and hold the pen higher and loosely, at first it seems unnatural, but this is really natural.

Oka said, 'When morality, *shila*, begins to become established in practice, it shows its fundamental nature,' (for the Sanskrit word *shila* means 'innate tendency'). 'It is not something that is imposed, but is one's innate tendency which has been veiled by bad constricting habits. When those habits have been resolved with some effort, then the natural tendency asserts itself.'

The Full Glory in Great Religions

The great religions of the world, if they are gone into, have a mystical side which is not far removed one from the other. It is also reasonable to say that in certain religions the full glory of some facet shows itself. For instance, in Christianity the full glory of service has shown itself. There is service in Buddhism, but not the great Orders of service, such as the Jesuit Order which has educated half the world (including many communists).

Again, it had never struck me, before a foreigner pointed it out, that many of our hospitals are named after saints—St Mary's, St Bartholomew's—which shows that originally they were religious foundations. So we can say that, in Christianity, the glory of service has really shown itself.

One of the glories that has shown itself in Buddhism is detachment in action, and another is the freedom, the transcendence of the limited sense of individuality, the limited 'I'. This is not original to Buddhism. We can find it in the Upanishads which are considerably before the time of the Buddha.

In the Brihadaranyaka-Upanishad it says: *The Self is not long, not short, not big, not small,* and lists many more negations . . . not anything that you can imagine . . . not thus . . . not so . . . Whatever you say—no, no, no.

Again, there is a lost Upanishad; it may be very ancient. It is known from just a few quotations. You will be familiar with the situation:

A man comes to the teacher and asks, 'How can I attain freedom?'

The teacher says, 'Learn to know the true Self.'

The man says, 'Teach me.'

But the teacher doesn't reply.

The man says again, 'Sir, teach me the true Self.'

And the teacher still sits silent, unmoving.

He says for the third time, 'Teach me the true Self'.

Then the teacher says, 'I do teach you, but you do not understand. Silent is this Self.'

If we look at a book of *koans* for warriors, one of them cites an old tradition: A great Brahmin came before the Buddha. He bowed and said, 'What do you teach?' The Buddha sat in silence. The great Brahmin made a deep bow and went away satisfied. Then Ananda said to the Buddha, 'What did he get, that he went away satisfied?' The Buddha answered, 'The good horse goes even at the shadow of the whip.' This was given as a kind of riddle to warriors around 1400 CE.

How is it that Ananda, the attendant of the Buddha, didn't understand? The Brahmin understood. What was it that he understood or experienced? Silent is this. There is noise, not just the external noise, but the noise of our thoughts, the noise of our feelings, the noise of the unresolved karmic impulses . . . But silent is this. There is something beyond the noise.

Regret

This is a recent story of two students in a provincial town in Iran:

The new government of the Shah was looking for young talent to promote into government and sent a minister to the provincial towns in order to recruit the brightest. Two very promising students had done exceptionally well and the minister was going to interview both of them, but he had only a day in the town and one of the students suddenly went down with an acute illness. Only one of them was therefore interviewed, and that one was taken to the capital to begin his new life.

For the one who went down with the illness, it was just bad luck. He was left behind. He wrote in his account many years later that he felt bitter, but made the best of it. He got on with his life and became a prominent man in the provincial town. And he did a certain amount of good, but . . ! He also followed his friend's career in its early stages as he was moved up under the minister's patronage, until he disappeared above the clouds, so to speak. He knew his former friend must have got some cracking job in the new government under the successful minister. In spite of the successes that he had and the service he knew he was doing, all his life he had the feeling that, if only he hadn't been ill, the minister would have taken them both and he too would have had a chance.

He had lost touch with his friend early on. Thirty years later he had to visit an official in the capital. Arriving unexpectedly early he thought he would get a haircut. Near the ministry there was a street of little shops, so he dropped in at the barber there. A very shabbily dressed man came in whom he seemed to recognize. When he looked hard he realized it was his friend, his former fellow student. 'What has happened to you?' he asked. His friend said, 'I did do well at the beginning, but then the minister made a mistake and would not admit to it. Someone had to be sacrificed and I was sacked. They found me a job as a clerk and they told me not to make a fuss or I might find myself in prison.'

So he had spent his life in the capital as a lowly clerk. His friend promised him a better job in the provincial capital on his return.

He wrote, 'I realized then that I had spent thirty years of my life envying something that didn't exist.' Despite all his successes in the provincial town there was always the thought, 'If only I could have gone with my friend to share his success in the capital.' But the success of his friend didn't exist; it was unreal. He wrote, 'My life was poisoned by envy of something that I had imagined.'

Mindfulness

It is a common view that mindfulness is thinking—*Now I'm walking. Now I'm talking. Now I'm not walking or talking, but just standing. Now I'm sitting down...* It is just like a running BBC commentary. But, as a matter of fact, words cannot describe these things. Words can never describe what you do when you walk. There is only the actual living experience. If you say 'walk', does that mean the toe comes down first, the heel comes down first, or the foot comes down flat? The living experience is awareness of it all, but words can never describe it.

Mindfulness in words—trying to make an internal commentary of what one is doing—is just a kind of illusion. It can be compared to putting into words something that cannot be put into words, and that is not at all what is meant by mindfulness. The best example that I know is in relation to music.

One of the reasons that people are so powerfully moved by music is that it does not have words. There are no words to describe, say, a study by Chopin. Suppose you try to describe the 'Revolutionary Study' in words: *There is a crash, then a growl down the scale, and then up the scale, and then down...* Actually, there are no adequate words to describe it. Many things in art can be put into words, but in music there are no words at all to describe it. This is one of the reasons it is so powerful.

Musicians themselves have words. When musicians hear music they automatically score the main theme in their heads, and if they have perfect pitch, they are uneasy until they have fixed it as A or B flat. They have words for the 'Revolutionary'; they would say: *It starts with a dominant seventh chord on G but in the first inversion, then there is a series of four-note descending passages, also the dominant with a leading-note accidental, and then there is a tremolo in the bass C and G.* So, there is something that they can say, but it doesn't really describe the music.

This can shed light on Buddhist teaching in practice because here too, in fact, there are no words. Musicians *know*, practitioners *know*, but trying to formulate it in words is not much better than trying to describe the 'Revolutionary Study' in words.

We can learn other things from music. You do not hang on to a chord, however beautiful. You do not regret the end of a piece of music. The piece is played and comes to a natural end. In the same way, a life is played.

In Beethoven's Sonata 107, the variations get higher and higher, faster and faster, but at the end of the rushing demisemiquavers, suddenly, the score says quasi-religioso, as if religious, and then comes a very, very quiet restatement of the theme, and it ends in silence.

We do not feel: *Oh, how tragic! All those wonderful notes, that tremendous dexterity, the speed, and now all he can play is this simple theme.* No, this is part of the sonata; it is not something to be regretted.

We are not supposed to give personal reminiscences in judo, but just as an example, I will tell you. I have been in the *Guinness Book of Records*. It was an enormous effort. Judo is very useful if you practise for up to four or five years. It tells you what to do if people start pushing; it tells you how to move the furniture and how to use your body generally. However, in the higher levels you practise special speed, balance, and dexterity in very rare techniques which are devised to overcome opponents who are also practising special speed, balance and dexterity in very rare techniques, and whom you never meet except on the contest mat.

The whole situation is entirely artificial. I suppose it does keep one fit, but fit for what? Nothing really. It takes all your time. It *is* nice to have your picture in the *Guinness Book of Records*, but it is nothing, it is absolutely unreal. Since the time I have not been able to move energetically, I get much more done. I am not spending hours each day cultivating something artificial. People think, How sad! He was so fit and well. Now he can't even walk thirty yards. No, it's much better now. I am not restless; I am not always wanting to jump over something. I can sit and study, write or think.

Casual Doubts

Casual doubts can be a problem. The mind dithers:

> Science does not believe in anything beyond the material effects to which everything can be reduced . . .
>
> Oh, but Einstein believed in a spiritual reality . . .
>
> Einstein lived a long time ago, you know.
>
> In 1970 Monod wrote *Chance and Necessity*—a very influential book, a very important book . . .
>
> But there are modern scientists like Paul Davis, for instance. They find a design in the universe . . .

This goes on endlessly. A casual doubt comes up . . . then it is challenged, and down it goes, but it comes up again in a new form. This is not the way to meet doubts, one by one. Taking a few days, one could consider the following:

> 1. Buddhism is an ancient tradition and so it knows the sort of thing that can happen.
>
> 2. It has a line of teachers who incorporate in themselves the experience of many centuries of practising these direct experiments on consciousness.

3. It is an experimental thing, experiments that the scientists do not make.

4. They never consider the observer, or haven't until the last twenty years or so. Buddhism makes experiments on the 'I'—the observer and consciousness.

5. It has a definite effect. If we look at history, for instance, the Buddhist India of Ashoka, the Mauryan dynasty, had become almost a heaven on earth. Even H.G. Wells, a sceptic, in his super-bestseller, *A Short History of the World*, reckons that the reign of Ashoka was one of the high points of human achievement. They had a welfare state, hospitals for animals, and the Greek ambassador reported that the rich could leave their houses open with no guards. If the people made an agreement, they kept their word; there were no written contracts. Those who did break their word were stigmatized and no one would do business with them again. People were honest and compassionate. The treatment in the human hospitals was based on three principles—cleanliness, kindness to the patients, and diet. Surprisingly modern, isn't it? We can say that Mahayana Buddhism is the greatest civilizing force that the world has ever known. It has this history of wonderful achievement.

6. And lastly, I have committed myself to this, and I am going through with it, doubts or no doubts.

Settle six points, like this, for example, in your mind.

At the court of Nobunaga, a warrior lord, there was an argument about training new recruits—the sword or the spear first? The sword master said that new recruits should be taught the sword first and then the spear. His argument was that the spearman has only one chance to nail the swordsman as he comes in. If that one spear thrust is deflected, the spear is absolutely useless at close quarters, and he will be cut to pieces by the sword.

Nobunaga inclined to this view himself, but asked the opinion of an able retainer named Hideyoshi. This was a man of the people, who had never trained in arms; nevertheless he gave his opinion, which was that training should begin with the spear. The sword master was furious, and proposed a test—a new recruit with one week's training at the sword against another with one week's training at the spear. Hideyoshi agreed but pointed out that this would be largely a test of two individuals, not of the weapons. He proposed twelve men with the sword, against twelve men with the spear, and this was agreed.

The test was to be this: one team was to be armed with light wooden swords, and the other team with wooden spears with a thick pad on the end. In addition, the spearmen would have a small wooden ball lightly tied onto the crown of the head. If a swordsman could knock off the ball, he would win; if the spearman could knock the swordsman over, he would win.

After the week's training, which was conducted in private, the two teams lined up facing each other before the whole court. At the signal, each swordsman began to advance towards the opponent facing him. But to everyone's surprise, the spearmen did not wait there, but rushed to the end of the line—six to the right-hand end and six to the left. They then advanced together towards the single swordsman at each end of the line—a wall of six spears. He could deflect only one of them and the other five immediately knocked him over. They advanced without check on the next man, and then the next, with the same instant result. By the time the bewildered remaining men could think of anything, they were themselves overwhelmed.

This is the way to meet doubts. Don't meet doubts with a single response. Meet a doubt with an array of six points that you have established in your mind, and then you will not be troubled by doubts.

Taking Refuge in the Sangha

There is support from the *sangha* (community), but it is very easy to start relying on that support and not contributing yourself.

There was a famine in India and the poor were badly off. So the local Brahmin placed a small tank in the middle of the village square and covered it with wet cloths to keep it cool. Then he asked all the well-off to bring a pot of milk during the day and pour it into the tank. In the evening he would then call the poor together and dispense it to them to ensure that they at least had a little milk.

That was agreed. But in the evening, when the Brahmin called the poor together and uncovered the tank, he found that there was nothing in it but water. Each householder had thought, 'The others will put in milk, so my pot of water won't make any difference.' There was no milk given at all.

It is very easy in a group to rely on the others.

There is a terrible Cornish proverb: *When twelve men turn a boat over—which is a big effort—one of them is foxing.* He is grimacing, but not doing the work; the others are doing it.

In the *sangha*, it is easy to think the others are working well. Despite the fact that I may do *something*, the full responsibility is on every member of the *sangha* to put in 'the *full* quota of milk'.

Studying the Holy Texts

It is worth knowing that if you have a bad character, you have to do a lot of study. This does not mean that everyone who studies has a bad character, but if you have a bad character and try to do good, what you do will usually be disastrous—you will take over things, you will boss people around, you will hate and destroy people who stand against you; it will be awful. If you study the holy texts, it will at least keep you out of mischief, which is a great advantage for the world! But you have to study properly.

As an example, most Christians know the parable of the sower. The sower went forth to sow and as he sowed, some of the seed fell on the wayside and the birds came and ate it up. Some fell among the stones, others among thistles, and some on the good soil. This is a riddle. The disciples asked Jesus, 'What does it mean? What is this sower doing? Why isn't he sowing on the good soil? What is he doing sowing among the stones and thistles? Look at the seed that fell on the wayside. The birds came and ate it up.' Just as the bird is a little bit stronger because of that, so those people of bad character who read the holy texts, can turn them to serve their own purposes. They can make use of them for prestige or to make money.

So we must not study like bird-people where the potential of the seed is completely lost. We must study under proper direction, and study so that the text enters us and manifests its potential.

On this point of keeping one out of mischief, my private demon or Mephistopheles comes—not too often now—and says, 'There's a chance to do them down. You've never liked them. Now is your chance.'

And I say, 'I haven't got time. I have to finish this off.'

He says, 'You've never got time. Last year you had a chance to put a spoke in the wheel and what did you do? Messing about with your texts!'

And I say, 'I can't do everything. Doing these texts, I haven't got time to do the things you're suggesting.'

He tends to say now, 'I'm not wasting my time on you!' and keeps away for quite a while. Study does keep one out of mischief! If we study the holy texts, gradually they will show something which is not actually in the texts themselves. We study them, and if we continue practising, we can become aware of something else. We read about suffering, and it becomes suffering . . . and something else. Sickness . . . and something else. Old age . . . and something else. Death . . . and something else.

The teacher who said this went on to say, 'I had better stop now, or you will have me in a lunatic asylum.'

Leaves and Moss

In some Japanese temples, moss is cultivated as a symbol of inner realization. Its progress cannot be forced, and the cultivation, in fact, amounts to removing the obstacles to the natural growth. If these are patiently and continuously got rid of, however, the moss makes a surprisingly rapid advance.

Moss, like realization, has a great inner strength against even extremes of change in the environment. Under very warm or very dry conditions mosses can become dormant, and quickly revive and grow again when conditions improve. If they feel like it, some of them can keep on growing even on hot, dry and exposed rocks. Most of them, however, grow best in shady and moist environments. In the temple gardens where they are cultivated, small trees are therefore planted which shed their leaves at different times of year, thus providing a certain amount of shade for the moss almost all the time.

A huge training temple like Eiheiji of the Soto Zen sect has a good number of courtyards covered with moss. One of the daily jobs is to weed out its competitors, and then to sweep the moss clear of fallen leaves. This is done with a light broom of twigs, and there is quite an art to it. If the strokes are too heavy, the surface of the moss is damaged, but if the strokes are not strong enough, the leaves are not taken up. So it has to be done just right. The piles of leaves are then put into sacks and burnt to help heat the bath. After the sweeping is over, unbroken lines of the undulating green carpet are a rewarding sight.

The job, however, may involve little irritations. When one is sweeping a courtyard, and the part that has been done is taking on its pristine appearance, a breeze dislodges a few more leaves. One goes back and picks them up, only to see a couple more redly blotting the ground somewhere else.

When I was first given a courtyard to sweep, I thought to myself, as foreigners tend to do, 'Well, I may not be as good as some of these professionals at sitting in meditation, and perhaps I don't always understand what's said to me, but this I can do, and I'll do it perfectly, absolutely perfectly.'

To me that meant sweeping every last leaf from the moss, as I had been asked to do. It was surprising, and then infuriating, to find that it seemed impossible to get the desired result. On the first day I left the place spotless, having made a last quick circuit picking up the few newly fallen leaves, but as I took the sack and turned to go, I saw a few more come down. There was no time to go back yet again.

I evolved a strategy which I tried out the next day. Before beginning to sweep, I visited each tree in turn and shook it furiously, in both senses of the word—I was then still fairly strong, and knew how to use my strength. Every leaf that was even beginning to weaken its hold on the tree came down in the shower with all the others. Then I happily swept them all up into piles, and put the piles into the sack. No leaves remained to defile the perfect carpet of green.

As I moved off triumphantly, I noticed a monk watching me. He said, 'Leggett-san, don't you think that was a bit extreme?'

I replied shortly, 'Well, it got all the leaves up.'

'Yes,' he said, 'But, you know, we sweep these places every day. If a few leaves come down after we've finished, we take them up the next day. And just a few of them might make an attractive pattern, don't you think?'

I remembered a Chinese poem: *One spot of red in a sea of green.* I don't know if he was referring to that .. ? Anyway, I suddenly felt a bit uncivilized.

So I stopped fighting the trees.

Years afterwards I came across a Japanese poem by a great master named Mamiya, written early in the twentieth century. The experience I had in mind helped me to appreciate it:

We sweep up the fallen leaves in the garden,
But we don't hate the trees for dropping them.

It doesn't apply only to leaves!

Help, No Help

Sometimes a new idea can change the whole landscape of endeavour, so that everything appears in quite a different light. This applies to most fields of human activity. But in the case of spiritual endeavours, it has some special overtones.

Take the case of doing certain jobs for the spiritual group, for example. Naturally, everyone would like to choose the job that they are good at. Someone good at adding would like to do the accounts, and someone good at gardening would like to help in the garden. But as the Christian saying has it: *A cross selected is no true cross.*

To do what one can do well where others can see it, is an assertion of personality, and it has not much value as a discipline, though the community may get some benefit from it. Even that benefit, however, is usually offset by the unconscious arrogance of the expert, perpetually putting others right, or taking things off their hands to do them better.

Reason-in-the-service-of-the-ego, or Mephistopheles, argues that it must be best to offer one's service in a field where one can make a really significant contribution. But while there is the feeling 'I am making a really significant contribution', training has not begun.

If all goes well, however, some students at least will begin to undertake things which they cannot do well, either at a suggestion from another person, or because they perceive a need—the accountant helps in the garden, perhaps enthusiastically cleaning the stones by scrubbing off moss that has been carefully cultivated for years, and appearing wantonly destructive; the gardener helps with the petty cash and gets the totals wrong, appearing . . . well, after all, where is the money going? Training has begun. Not easy. But, then, no one ever said it would be.

The service is undertaken in a spirit of offering. For a time it may bring a sort of self-sacrificing joy, but usually it becomes a consciously performed act of dedication to an unpleasant or, at least, a boring task. The performers see their time out, and then quit with a feeling of: *Well done, thou good and faithful servant!*

But, if all still goes well, the day comes when the landscape changes. To give a concrete example: The cushions of two sorts were kept in a large cupboard in one corner of a training hall. There were meetings of different kinds with different arrangements of the cushions. So, shortly before a meeting, they were all brought out and arranged in four big piles against one of the walls. Then the arrangers could easily take them and lay them out. To make these preliminary piles was the job of one fairly new member of the *sangha* (community). It was also his job to put them away afterwards.

One day, when a meeting had just ended, he was told by a senior that there was to be another meeting of a different and unusual kind in half an hour. He stood irresolute. As the senior looked at him, he said, 'There's no real point in putting them in piles just for ten minutes, is there? It will be just as easy for people to rearrange them from where they are; probably a lot of them will stay put.'

'Have we something else to do?' asked the other.

'Well, could you tell me something about what came up in the sermon the other day, about the Buddha who lives for a thousand years and the other Buddha who lives for only one day?'

'Yes, certainly,' said the senior, 'and there's also a Buddha who lives for only ten minutes,' and he began to pick up the cushions and stack them into the usual piles. The two worked together in silence, and in ten minutes the cushions were in their piles perfectly aligned against the wall in the bare hall. They stood back and looked at them, and the senior remarked, 'He lives only ten minutes, but now his life has had its meaning.' Then the other assistants came in and began to take them down to rearrange them.

The moment of looking at the cushions seemed to stand out in the mind of the junior—the cushions, brilliantly clear, as if they had been in a shaft of sunlight. After that he did not feel impatient with small chores, or think, 'Is it really worth doing?' He felt each time: *The Buddha lives only so long... Now his life has been fulfilled.* He felt the Buddha in himself. And then, gradually, it went off. He could sometimes revive it by recalling that first moment, but slowly it disappeared as a living inspiration.

This kind of thing very often happens, and people on a spiritual path become familiar with it. Sometimes they get vaguely resentful, and even embittered. When they feel a stir of spiritual life in them, Mephistopheles whispers: *Remember how many times this has happened before, and remember how it all went off afterwards. Like a little drug, isn't it? You feel better for a bit, but then it goes off and there's a reaction, and life is even greyer than before.* There are those who, under the pressure of these insinuations, give up making serious efforts.

In the same way, a spiritual incident, or a text perhaps, can be a great inspiration for a time, but if it remains only an idea, the effect wears off. After that, to keep running it over in the mind is like a good-luck charm without living effect. The ideas are not useless; they can be a great help, and, for many, an absolute necessity in waking up inner inspiration and energy. But to rely on these fixed things as a substitute for inner life will always lead to disappointment. They are pools, even lakes, whereas what is wanted is a bubbling spring.

Willow

The poem reads:

PATIENT ENDURANCE

> *Winds may come*
>> *that are not pleasant—*
> *The willow!*

This poem is not to be read as an indication that there are storms before which any resistance is useless, so that we must be prepared for hopeless suffering.

The willow branches are indeed whirled about by the will of the wind, but its root remains firm. There is a firm calmness at the root of the mind which can be culti-vated, and the poem is a hint. The lower of the two large Chinese characters represents a sword-blade across the heart, showing that the adverse winds are not merely outer circumstances. But they pass, and the willow-root remains, unshaken even by a tempest which can up-root a great oak.

The Space Within the Heart

These short pieces are here presented on the basis of their effectiveness, without theoretical justification. They are like the lime juice with which the Scottish naval surgeon in 1753 was curing the often fatal scurvy among British sailors, centuries before Vitamin C or its deficiency had been heard of. The lime juice worked. Some of these pieces, too, can work, and that is the point of presenting them, not to attempt to explain them from a theoretical point of view. They are just isolated pieces, and the hope is that one or two of them may get the reaction.

Sukha-Duhkha, *Pleasure-Pain*

This is the first piece. We hear of two words a lot in Indian thought—*sukha* (pleasure and happiness), and *duhkha* (sorrow or pain). These are familiar words in Buddhism, but there is a secret in them. *Sukha* comes from *su*, meaning 'good' and *kha* meaning 'space'. *Duhkha* comes from *dus* (or *duh, dur, dush* and so on, depending on the next syllable of the Sanskrit compound) meaning 'bad', and *kha*, 'space'. The origin of the words, with their sense of happiness or pleasure and sorrow or distress, comes from the application to the axle of a chariot. As you know, the axle goes through the centre of the wheel as it turns. Now *su-kha* 'good space' is when there is space so that the wheel can turn freely on the axle, and *duh-kha* 'bad space' is when there is not enough space, or when the space is uneven or gritty, so that wheel and axle grind against each other, or stick and don't move smoothly.

Sukham as an adverb can also mean ease. For instance, *sukham-asit* refers to someone sitting at ease. So, when there is space at the axle to move easily, the chariot will go forward smoothly and happily. The hint from the make-up of these two words is that in our actions, in our interchanges with the world, we need to have a little space. If the world and the events, and the circumstances outer and inner, press too directly on us, we can't move easily within them, especially if there's a lot of grit and it's too tight anyway. But if we can learn to make a little space, then our actions, and our thoughts, can move easily without obstruction.

This is a hint that we can learn to make a little space in life, and it is done by practice. How? Suppose we are doing some job, a wearing job. We can learn to break off completely for a few seconds. We put it down so to speak, close the eyes if we are alone, and sit up. Then we can take in a slow, deep breath, and on the out-breath feel the muscles and nerves relax into empty space. Perhaps it takes thirty seconds. Then we take up the job again.

This is one of the first points—to make a little space, to get the habit of trying to make that little space. Then, even when I am furiously angry . . ! Suppose someone hits me, I feel my body moving into reaction. But if I've cultivated the habit of a little space, in the middle of my anger I find myself taking a deep breath and my nerves relaxing momentarily. After those few seconds I then go to take up anger again... but something in me says, 'Oh, I don't know . . . what do I care anyway?' and I find, to my surprise, that I really don't care. There has been a tiny break, and the anger has not been transmitted so automatically across that break.

These things have to be practised regularly. There is no time to philosophize or think of little spaces at a time of anger, or temptation, or fear. If we have practised in the ordinary way, then we shall find, to our surprise, that when one of these things hits us and we are about to make our typical reaction, there is somehow just a little space within us, and we're free from our usual automatic responses. So this was the hint from the derivation of the words *sukha* and *duhkha*.

Kannon-with-a-Thousand-Arms

Now the second piece concerns a nobleman in the feudal days of Japan who had a responsible position. He developed a great respect for a certain fencing master and thought he would like to take up fencing himself. The teacher accepted this keen pupil, and after some time the pupil became an expert. He entered the grading contests and won most of them. The teacher then told him, 'You are now master of the sword, and I will give you the diploma of mastership.'

The pupil was delighted to receive the diploma, but after a while he came back to the teacher. He said, 'There is something wrong. This is not what I expected.'

'You asked to learn fencing and you have the diploma and you are worth it,' replied the teacher.

'No. When I'm in the fencing hall facing an opponent, I have confidence, but outside the fencing hall it's different. I'm not like you. You have confidence outside the fencing hall, but I haven't got that.'

'You asked me to teach you fencing,' the teacher said.

'Yes, but can you teach me to be like you?'

'No. I can teach up to the diploma. I can give you the technical skill and you have that, but now the Way has to be found by you yourself.'

We won't go into the difficulties he had, but this

account gives a hint. There is a *bodhisattva* (enlightened being) called Kannon in Japan, and Kuan-yin in
China. In the Far East this being is often represented
in feminine form, so it has been compared to Mary
the Madonna. There is one big difference, however.
Although it is a compassionate mother figure, in the
Far East it is never shown as mother and child. The
normal representation is of a feminine figure radiating compassion and wisdom. The *bodhisattva* is also
sometimes shown possessing many arms, like some
of the Indian gods, and is often called Kannon-with-a-
thousand-arms, or even with-a-thousand-eyes.

Some Western critics deride these figures: *A thousand arms, a thousand eyes! This is a rather primitive
representation to symbolize omnipotence and omnis-
cience. But these distortions of the human form are
quite distasteful.* Such critics show that they haven't
the faintest idea of the point of such Kannon figures.
It is, of course, true that they do hint at something
glorious. Buddhists have a doctrine of Buddha-
in-glorious-form; there is *sambhogakaya* (body of
delight), *nirmanakaya* (body of transformation). The
Buddha-nature also manifests in every grain of sand
and everything—action or thought. Buddha-nature
appears in different forms, and one form is glory. But
there is another which you can see in the everyday
incidents of ordinary life. The thousand arms show
that this *bodhisattva* can manifest in any of the forms,
can manifest in the things and actions of everyday
life. Again, it is teaching that we must turn away from

being totally absorbed in the presumed reality of things, and just turn back to find a Kannon in ourselves. The fencing pupil with his diploma had one arm, so to say, but away from the sword, he had nothing.

We can think, 'Well, I'll get more arms, more skills.' Most of us have particular ways of meeting the world—some of us by shouting and domineering, and some of us by saying, 'Of course I'm no good at anything like that. You'll have to help me,' which is just as much a technique as being aggressive. There are various techniques, but we get stuck in one or two, and don't know how to use even these appropriately. You need a *bodhisattva* to do that. Until the *bodhisattva* is awakened, even thousands of techniques, skills and advantages of money will all be inappropriate. They won't save us. When the Kannon is awakened, then all these things can be used in the right way, appropriately, in accord with the nature of conditions. In this case, the fencing pupil practised going beyond the sword-skill, and finally attained what they call the sword-of-no-sword.

Such a story, with its happy ending, sounds all right, but the question is: What is the actual practice? Although it is not desirable to talk too much about personal things, you are allowed to do so sometimes, in cases where experience gives conviction. In judo, which I can say I know, even experts generally rely on two or three things in which they have special skill.

Of course, they know a great many, but it is by those few that they get the results, and even of those few, there is one in which they have specialized and maybe found something new. The time comes when a promising student has an exchange with a traditional teacher, who says to him just before a contest, 'How are you going to win this?'

'I'll make a few feints to find out his reactions, and then I'll come in with my *toku-i*, my special one, accordingly.'

'Give up the thought, "This is how I'm going to win."'

'Then how can I win?'

'Don't try to win. Go out with nothing in your mind.'

Not many of us have the courage or faith to try this at once. But we do try it on lesser occasions. The first time, you go out 'with nothing in mind, practising inner training, transcending all techniques', and you find yourself flat on your back. Something in you grumbles, 'Doesn't work, does it? I thought it wouldn't,' and some give up then and there.

But others may persist. It's called cutting off the bull's horns. The horns are what the bull fights with, and your special technique is what you fight with. It's not only in judo; it may be a technique of domineering, or pathetic helplessness.

The practice of cutting off, in judo, is giving up

ideas of that *toku-i*, that special trick, or any other technique. You throw it away. Gradually, you begin to find that the body can take care of itself against an opponent, and you get a little confidence. Then, one day, something happens—no one knows what it will be—and now it is *he* that is flat on his back, and you don't quite know how it happened.

Then there may be tremendous excitement, and you think, 'A-a-a-ah! Now I'll do it again!' But, no! The mind is not empty now, it is packed with anticipation of another triumph. So it doesn't work again. All that has got to be thrown away into space, into emptiness. This is the judo-of-no-judo.

Illusions

The third piece derives from Iida Toin, a Soto Zen master of the early twentieth century. He remarked that the world runs mainly on illusions. Now, high-level statements like this are frightfully interesting and sound wonderful, but as they stand they are of no use to you. There is a way of saying inwardly: 'Yes, yes, that's the transcendental truth of course,' and then turning back to what you still regard as the *real* world!

The way to make use of statements like this from Iida is to keep an eye open for how they work in daily life. He was not talking about transcendental truth, but of the business of this world before our eyes. Here is an example which I encountered some years ago:

A Hungarian actor-director had managed to get out of Hungary before the roof fell in there, and came to Britain. He had a good appearance, was always smartly dressed, and was a former Olympic fencer. When he arrived, his English wasn't really good enough for the stage. It was excellent, with no mistakes, but he couldn't yet manage the nuances necessary. So he looked for a job, and he told me, 'I became an efficiency expert.'

'How did you come to know about that?' I said.

'I didn't, I just presented myself and talked to them for a bit, using some of the words I had learnt.'

'But how could you act the job like that?'

'I wasn't an efficiency expert, but I *was* an actor. I simply acted the efficiency expert.'

'But they must have found out almost at once.'

'Oh, they did, but I wasn't sacked. They found I was very useful to them. You see, the real efficiency expert doesn't look like one. He's thinking about the measurements of movement and motion and flows and all that, but his tie is never in the middle, he's got odd socks on, and his shoes aren't polished. He's a scientist and he can't be bothered to dress carefully. He doesn't look the part.

'So they used to send us out in pairs, with me as the senior, looking like a real efficiency expert. The real one would shamble in untidily after me, as my assistant. The clients would put their problems to me, and I would look at my assistant and say, "Got that?" He would do all the work, and at the very end, I would present the report and they'd be very satisfied.'

This is an example of what Iida was talking about when he said the world runs mainly on illusions. The efficiency experts don't look like what they are imagined to be like, so an illusion has to be provided. If we keep our eyes open we can see how often this happens. He says that the world is full of illusions, and in a sense everything in the world is behind a mask, and what's behind it is not the same as what the mask is showing.

This is the first point of the teaching, but it goes much further than that. Some of us get good at seeing behind the masks of the world, but that is not the real problem. The real problem is that I myself am wearing a mask which is hiding what I really am. Iida says, 'Turn within, turn within.' I must find what is behind my own mask of thoughts, memories, feelings, habits, intentions and ambitions. All these form a mask which is constantly changing; all the time it is changing. If the needle-point of meditation—as one teacher called it—can penetrate through the mask, I can find something that doesn't change with the changing of the mask.

Iida says that it is not good to try to specify these things too exactly, but it can be called a little glimpse of immortality in this very life. No one comes back from beyond the grave to tell us whether there is a soul or not, but one can have an experience in this very life, and when death comes, one nods and says, 'I've been here before.' Iida tells us that if we can penetrate through the mask in our meditation, we can find this treasure for ourselves.

There are other examples of common illusions which have an application to Buddhism. When we were children at the seaside, we used to look at the waves going across in front of us. When we are small, we think that the top of the wave is a *thing,* a bit of water which is travelling along on the surface of the sea. If we think back, we may remember our first surprise when we saw something like a cork which did not go along as part of the wave, but just bobbed up and down as each wave passed. It took a little time to realize that the wave was not a thing, as we had thought. We know now that the wave is not that solid thing, and yet it still makes sense to talk about 'a wave' when explaining radio to children. That is one example.

Another is to compare our internal changes to clouds. You look up at the sky and see mostly clouds. This means that there is light somewhere apart from them and you notice a little patch of blue. When you are small, you think this is another cloud—a blue one. Sometimes the blue cloud gets bigger as do the others, and sometimes it gets smaller. It may divide into two or more, or it may vanish, leaving only the grey and white clouds. Yet the truth is, the patch of blue is not a thing in the same way as a cloud is a thing. In ourselves, that blue—Iida Toin rather reluctantly calls it universal consciousness—is not a thing as the clouds of our thoughts, feelings, convictions, conscious and unconscious, are things. There is a famous poem, by a devotee of the Pure Land sect:

> Do not think, 'It is clearing up now and soon
>   it will be bright.'
> From the very beginning, in the sky,
>   was always the brightness of the moon.

The poem is telling us not to think that the clouds alternate with brighter periods in our minds. From the very beginning, behind and beyond the clouds, illuminating them, is the brightness of the Buddha-nature.

The various Ways have their own illustrations of Zen principles which may be puzzling when indicated merely by words. For instance, we are told: *When you see, hear, or touch, think what it is that you are seeing or hearing or touching. It is the Buddha-nature. These things are all the same.* People say, or at any rate think to themselves, 'But that's ridiculous. They're all quite different. When all the quick talking has died down, they're not the same.' The Zen master Shaku Soyen used to say that individuals are many, but considered as a nation, they are one. Judo has its own illustration, which is perhaps more vivid:

> *A fist is brandished. What's that? A fist and nothing else.*
>
> *Now, from the clenched fist, a thumb is stuck out. What's that? A thumb.*
>
> *Then, from a fist, a straight index finger points. What's that? A finger.*
>
> *Now, the fully opened hand is held up. What's that? A hand.*

So there are these separate things which are not the same—fist, thumb, finger, hand. Yet, as a matter of fact, they *are* all the same, namely—hand. Still, when a fist is held up, we don't call it a hand, we say 'fist'. Stretch the fingers, though, and the fist vanishes and becomes a hand, which it always was.

Words of Love

Iida remarked once: *Words of love are not always kindly words.* Let us look at a specific case. Suppose I've never been healthy, and my general physical condition is getting worse and worse. No serious illness yet, but I recognize that I have to do something about it; my life situation demands that I get well quickly. So I put myself in the hands of an expert who gives me a programme which includes an early morning run followed by a cold shower and all sorts of restrictions on diet and late nights. The body grumbles: *Oh no! I can't stand this!* or, *Oh, not that again!* and *Can't we have just one day off?* and so on. The programme has to be imposed on the body, imposed by force. The body finds it hateful. But the basis is love, and after a few months the body is grateful for the new vigour and zest in physical movement.

There is a Japanese poem that says if the mother loves the child, then when she slaps it it is right, and when she gives it a sweet it is right, and when she ignores it it is right, and when she makes a fuss of it, that too is right. But if it is a stepmother who secretly hates the child, then when she slaps it it is wrong, when she gives it a sweet it is wrong, when she ignores it, that is wrong, and when she makes a fuss of it, that too is wrong.

We have to realize that life cannot be always easy and pleasant. Suppose there is a child who is very talented musically and is studying the piano under a good teacher. It is not always going to be pleasant. The child wants to play, it is true, but not scales. The child wants to play the waltzes of Strauss or Gungl, but not Bach or Beethoven. Some force has to be used, but that force is based on insight and love, not of the unformed taste of the child, but of the talent that is awaiting development.

Doing Good as Against Not Doing Harm

My impression is that there is a difference between typical Eastern and Far Eastern attitudes, and typical Western ones. Take a case given by the Chinese Zen master Tozan. You see a hungry snake pursuing a frog. What do you do? Not liking snakes, you get a stick and beat off or maybe kill it. You save the frog, and the frog immediately goes on to catch flies on its long sticky tongue. On the other hand, suppose you don't interfere. Then the snake will eat the frog, and the flies will be safe, at least from that frog. So if you interfere, the snake loses, the frog does well, and the flies lose. If you don't interfere, the snake does well, the frog loses, and the flies do well. That is two to one. So you do better by not interfering.

And I feel that most of the rules in the *vinaya* and other Eastern moral codes are negative: *Don't kill. Don't slander people. Don't get drunk. Don't harm people (ahimsa).*

Compare this with the so-called golden rule: *What you would like others to do to you, do that to them.* Jesus is reputed to have said this. But some years before Jesus, lived the great Rabbi Hillel who, as a matter of fact, anticipated a few of the sayings attributed to Jesus! He was asked by some idiot, 'Can you sum up the whole of the Law while I stand on one leg?' Now, most people cannot stand on one leg for more than a few seconds, but Hillel told him, 'Yes.' So this man stood on one leg, and Hillel said, 'Don't do to others what you wouldn't want them to do to you. That is the Law. All the rest is commentary.'

Don't harm them, he was saying. He wasn't saying do positive good to them. This latter, of doing positive good, has been criticized on the grounds that my idea of positive good, namely, what I should like for myself, may not be the same as your idea of positive good. When Einstein was young, he used to feel lonely, and he would have liked people to come and talk to him. But later on in life, he was saying, 'The great boon is to be *alone.*' If someone had seen him then, that person might have thought, 'I like being talked to, so old Einstein would like that now,' and gone on *chattering, chattering, chattering.*

I have suggested that many of the precepts are negative—not to do harm. But it is not simply that. A person concerned with not doing harm is setting an example of peace and calm, and because of that calm, that person can see more clearly what is harm and what is not harm. Too often, one who is doing what one regards as positive good is setting an example of extreme agitation and, consequently, not very good insight.

Practice

Now a word about practice. We can have ideas and then practise, but practice has to be done till it goes past practice, until it is no longer practice. This is an example I heard from a master I knew. It was around the beginning of the twentieth century. The master happened to be in the place where the maids were doing the laundry. They were doing it as they did in Japan then. They soak the washing in the suds and then put it on a board and hit it with their fists. That knocks the dirt out. In India they used to swing a garment high and smash it down on a stone; effective but not so good for the garment in the long run. The master saw the maids doing this, and he stopped them and gave them a lesson in using the edge of the hand instead of the fists. He showed them how to strike with the force of the whole body rather than just with the arms. After that, he would go to look at them every month or so, and correct the movement when necessary. They became expert at it.

One day one of the girls had to go across Tokyo to visit a parent who was sick. It was thought that she would get back before sunset, but the visit took longer than expected and she had to come back in the dark. She kept to the lighted street but, as she passed in front of a dark alley, some roughneck jumped out and caught her long sleeve. Before she could think or panic, her arm and body moved in the familiar laundry stroke, and the edge of her hand broke his arm.

In a case like this, there is no idea of: *What am I going to do?* or even *How can I defend myself?* Her practice of the stroke had gone beyond practice. It was part of her, and when the need came, it was there. That teacher gave it as an example of how things should be practised: *Practise till it is no longer practice but a natural movement. Then, in a crisis, there is a sort of calm, an inner calm, a sort of coolness inside.*

A point about the difference between repetition and true practice: We can become experts in the holy texts. Then we can recite them, and they are true and wonderful. But if we do only this, we may become like certain chess players who learn many sequences of opening moves, sometimes up to move twelve or so. When you play against unknown opponents, they may be one of these. You can find them playing fine moves rapidly and confidently. You play very cautiously, because you seem to be up against a champion. Then they make a brilliant move which you have never seen before, and you realize that already, at move twelve, they have established a big advantage. You resign yourself to a long defensive battle. But then, on move thirteen, to your amazement they make an absolutely pointless move, and then another. You realize that they don't understand their own powerful position. They've got it, but they don't know what to do with it. They have been playing with other people's heads, so to speak, but now they have to use their own, and they don't know how to do it.

In the same way, a teacher has said: *You can learn religious ideas without actually understanding how to release the power that is in them. You haven't got access to their inner power.*

Only One Way

It is worth knowing that one can get hypnotized into thinking that there is only one way to do a thing correctly—it's the Right Way, and there are no other ways.

At All-India Radio, where I worked for a time, I used to see Indian violinists. My father was a professional violinist, one of the best of his generation. He led at the Covent Garden Opera for several years, and for a good time after that for Sir Thomas Beecham. So, I felt I knew something about violin playing. I was watching an Indian violinist in an AIR studio, playing in the orthodox way with the violin tucked under his left chin. It is axiomatic that the instrument must be held firmly in that way. At the very beginning, a pupil is made to hold the instrument like this, and even to take away the supporting left hand. The instrument has to remain sticking out there, held firmly by the pressure of the chin. It has to be absolutely steady, supported between the chin and the bent left arm, because the movements of the left-hand fingers are the fastest precise movements that can be made by humans—sometimes sixteen changes in a second. Unless there is absolute steadiness, it cannot be done.

The Indian violinist that I was watching seemed pretty good, and then he suddenly shocked me by laying the instrument along his extended left arm, still managing fast finger-work with the left hand. My whole musical experience rose in inner protest: *No, no! You can't do that!* But he was doing it and still playing effectively. As I was beginning to recover, he got bored with that little miracle, and stood the violin upright on his thigh, playing it at full speed like a little cello. I felt a . . . *can't do that, can't*, from inside. Then I gave up.

Later, I recalled something which my father had said in passing. He had learnt to hold very firmly with the chin, and he said that it was necessary in order to acquire the technical skill. But he added that in his private opinion, once mastery had been attained, it would be best to hold the violin as loosely as possible, so that the vibrations of the body of the violin are not muffled, as they must be to some extent with a tight hold. My memory is that he hinted that he thought a few violinists had discovered this for themselves, and that one of them had perhaps been Mischa Elman who hit the London musical scene at the beginning of the twentieth century. He was famous for his 'Elman tone' as, in a smaller way, my father had been famous.

I remember reading about Elman's first appearance in the West, in London I think. Several famous violinists came to hear this new star on the horizon. Among them was Jan Kubelik with a pianist friend. Kubelik was an established luminary, and he sat unmoving in the box as the wonderful Elman tone stretched out over the auditorium. As the applause rang out, he turned to his friend and remarked, 'Hot in here, isn't it?'

'Not for pianists!' came the reply.

Illusion Has No Parts

It may seem that an illusion gets thinner and finally fades away after quite some time. But in fact it is the reaction that gets thinner. The illusion, as such, goes all at once. It can take quite some time to get over the idea that everyone in uniform is *ipso facto* a bully and tyrant, or that every Armenian, Jew, or Parsee is by nature a subtle businessman. Dispelling big illusions, too, usually takes quite some time. But in all these cases some striking counterexample can bring the whole belief system down like a pack of cards. *Because* it is an illusion, it can go suddenly at any moment.

In a Tibetan version of the life of the Buddha, there is an interesting passage in one book in which a great Indian teacher made a striking comment. The original passage describes how Mara, king of the demons, set a demon called Red-Eye to keep watch on the Bo tree, under which, it was prophesied, the *bodhisattva* (enlightened being) would make his bid for Buddhahood. This demon was to report anything unusual.

For centuries Red-Eye watched the people coming and going past the Bo tree, but he saw nothing disturbing. Then, one day, he rushed away and presented himself before Mara, in a state of agitation. 'What is it?' asked Mara. The demon Red-Eye told him, 'My Lord, I have seen hundreds and thousands of people coming and going near the Bo tree, but saw nothing to report. Now there is a man walking towards that tree, and from the way he walks, I believe that whatever that man sets out to do, he will do. Let Your Majesty beware of what is taking place.'

The Indian teacher's comment was this: *Normally we do our spiritual practices, and we approach our meditation seat like all those people—the hundreds and thousands seen coming and going round the Bo tree. But the time will come—perhaps when we have a terrible disappointment, or fear, or great temptation—when we must become like that man walking towards the Bo tree, walking in a way that shows whatever he sets out to do, he will do. When you go to your meditation seat and sit for the meditation, normally you are thinking that it is a patient process of years. But, remember, all this is an illusion, and because it is an illusion, it can go at any time. Walk to your meditation cushion like the Buddha-to-be walking towards the Bo tree, saying: Today! Today! Today!*

East and West

This remarkable work, still preserved in Japan, is by an Indian priest who lived in fourteenth century China. His name was Indara, and he mastered the Chinese Zen painting, with its extreme economy of line.

The picture represents the meeting between the Zen monk Chih-chang, who succeeded the Sixth Patriarch at his temple, and the famous poet Chang Chi who held high ministerial rank.

A related poem reads:

Loving the Buddha, saintly men go to the holy West;
Averse to the Buddha, Bodhidharma turns his back
*   and comes to the East.*
They met in the tea-house of Illusion,
Dozing there, they lived through the dream.

Triumph and Success

One teacher said that people in the world aim at triumph, but spiritual people aim at success. You can spend as much time and energy on securing your triumph beyond your success, as you spent in getting the success.

You want to achieve something and it is achieved, but beyond that, you want acclamation, you want triumph, you want the people who opposed you to be humbled and humiliated, you want the Roman triumph where the captors were driven in front and the spoils were displayed—that is triumph! And the teacher said that this spoils the action. The action is no longer pure; it is polluted and corrupted by the desire for triumph. If this is lurking in the heart, then our actions will not be fruitful. They may seem to be effective, but in fact they are contaminated.

A very good example of this is in the life of the Emperor Nero. A scholar will say that probably the best ten years for people in the Roman Empire were the first eight or ten years of Nero's reign. You think, 'What?' When Nero was young, his tutor was Seneca, the first of the great Spanish thinkers, a Stoic philosopher. The country was ruled extremely well. Nero was a sensitive, artistic man. He wanted to replace the bloody Roman triumphs by triumphs of art and music. When he had to sign a death sentence, he said, 'Oh, I wish I'd never learnt to write.' Under Seneca's influence, he passed a law which set slaves free from torture. If a slave was tortured by his master, the magistrate had him compulsorily sold to another master. So this was the best time of the Roman Empire. But it was the same Nero—this gentle, artistic, compassionate man—who, after ten or twelve years, was taking part in the tortures himself—because the heart and the mind were not purified.

We can be full of good will, compassion and kindness. If we are in the position of an emperor, we can put these things into practice, and we do. But we have no defence against the corruption of the heart from within. There is a Japanese poem:

> Alas, it is the flower of the heart which fades,
>   without any outward sign.

We do not realize these things are happening to us. Without spiritual practice and discipline, gradually, even our best intentions and good deeds change. From success, we turn to seeking triumph and, consequently, the humiliation of others, conquest and glory.

The Reverence of Others

The doctrine is that the things of the world are not absolutely real, as we know. They have practical efficacy, and they have practical effects on us, but they are not absolutely real in themselves. And regularly, every few years, some clever dick comes along and says, 'Well, you know, all these holy texts and sacred utterances—they're all unreal, aren't they?' And, sure enough, you put this to a teacher. And the teacher says, 'Yes, yes.'

So the man says, 'Well, why do you use them then?'

This is a modern teacher, so he says, 'Well, I'm throwing imitation pearls to people who have got the idea that they are swine. They're rooting about in the mud, looking for some gold coins that they think they've lost. Now, when I throw them these imitation pearls, they suddenly feel, "Oh, we're rich!" and they stop looking around in the mud. Then they look around and realize that they're human beings! The imitation pearls make them feel better and it enables them to stop, to look around, and to realize what they are.'

A man visited a group and heard a text read. He returned to his own group afterwards and the teacher said, 'Well, did you benefit from the visit?'

The man said, 'It upset me a bit.'

The teacher said, 'Why was that?'

The man said, 'Well, the texts were read, and they were intoned, and there was a very strong atmosphere, but it was done without any reverence. Here we have always been taught reverence. So, I don't know . . . '

'What was the effect on you?'

'Well, I was put off by that. But I must admit that the resonance of those texts has remained with me; it did have an effect on me.'

And the teacher said, 'Good! While we're separated from the texts, we revere them and reverence is of utmost importance, but if it should happen that people become one with the texts, then it is not a question of uttering them with reverence. The texts are speaking the text, and there is no question of reverence; the texts are declaring themselves to the world, and it is an expression of truth.'

A lot of the old temples have treasures and, periodically—sometimes once a year—the treasures are brought out and exposed, and the public can go and see them. They are put in glass cases and some monk learns by heart the description of what the figure or treasure is. It may be a rare manuscript by the founder of the sect, or perhaps it is a relic of some kind.

I was in a little group trekking around, and we stopped in front of one of these cases. We were told by the monk what it was, and we looked. Then we moved on to the next case. And he stood again in front of this one and explained what it was, and then he happened to look at us and saw that we were looking at him! He turned around and noticed that the glass case was empty! And he said, 'Oh, it's gone away!' So we went on to the next case.

Now, this was used as an example of what can happen when the inner life of a movement begins to depart. You carry on as if it was still there, and there is a sort of convention of not asking questions about it. Some people, as in the case of the emperor's clothes, say, 'Oh, yes, yes, it's quite . . .' and then they move on. It can happen. The teacher said, 'Things can go on under their own momentum for quite a long time, long after the central experience has gone. And it has to be watched very carefully.'

Hakuin said that you can have a lot of trees with interlaced branches. The roots wither, but the trees support each other. It's like a table with many legs, but there is no actual 'life' because the roots have withered. They don't fall down; they are holding each other.

'Then,' Hakuin said, 'when a storm comes, the whole thing falls down!' He said, 'In the same way, people can support themselves on what they think is the reverence of others.' The others seem to be full of devotion and reverence, yet they may not feel anything in themselves. People see them behaving with apparent reverence and deference to these holy things and they think, 'They must believe; they are so reverent!' Actually, it may be that nobody believes in it at all, that we are all supporting each other on the behaviour of the rest of the group. Hakuin said that this gives the illusion there is still something living within it when it has long since gone away.

A Hundred Hearings, Not Like One Seeing

This is a Chinese phrase: *A hundred hearings are not like one seeing.*

We are all familiar with the experience of a trip to some famous place which we have heard and read about quite a lot. When we get there, it is different from what we expected. The hearings are not like one seeing. It is not that the hearings are wrong, necessarily, but they are incomplete. When we see, we understand what we have heard, sometimes for the first time.

Now, one of the things said is that you can learn by instruction, by hearing, or you can learn by seeing others, by observation, or you can learn by inference, or, finally, you can learn by experience yourself. And they say that you need all four for your final experience to be fruitful.

If you take them separately, you may say, for instance, 'Oh, let people find out for themselves.' But you can hear instruction that it is dangerous to drive when you are drunk. You can have observation—see that other people do this and they have serious accidents. Again, you can infer that it is a generally dangerous practice. If you are still so stupid that you have to have experience, you get drunk, you drive yourself, and you have a serious accident. The only point is that you may not be able to learn from the experience because you may be dead!

On the other hand, if the four ways of learning are taken in turn—first the instruction which corresponds to the text or the words of a teacher, and then the confirmation of that to some extent by observation, and the confirmation, again, by inference, and finally, the confirmation by direct experience—then that direct experience is fruitful because it has been directed through the instruction which was given at the beginning, which is from a fruitful source.

People say, 'Oh well, science has replaced all this. Science begins with observation.' Well, it doesn't begin with observation. Long ago they had a cartoon in an American army paper: The patrol gets lost. So the sergeant says to one of them, who is appropriately named Zero, 'Zero, climb to the top of that tree, and see what you can see.' He hopes for a sighting of a river or a mountain. Zero, who is fairly athletic, goes to the top of the tree. The sergeant calls, 'What can you see?' And Zero says, 'There is a bird's nest here, sir, but no eggs in it, and there are a lot of little caterpillars eating the leaves . . . '

That is observation. But it is not directed observation. Science has to begin with an idea, and then to observe on the lines of that idea in order to confirm it, or to develop it, or reject it.

Here is an example of how to apply observation—examples are best when they are striking—one can read about it and can agree internally. Sometimes you have a spiritual fall—you have a great temptation, and you fall. Or, you have a wave of anger, and you fall. Afterwards, there is regret, repentance and remorse. Well, I saw something once which made an impression on me. For you it is only something you are reading about, but still it is very vivid, it may be unexpected, and it can be a reinforcement. In the old days of judo, we used to have a big contest area of mats. Some of the seniors who had graduated from the university were not in the teams, but they came to support the event. They would take off their shoes and just sit round the edge of the mats in their ordinary clothes.

You are told in judo not to save a fall in a particular way; it is very risky. But we were, perhaps, risky fellows then. I saw a chap do it, and the elbow was dislocated as he went down. A man from the front row of the audience shot out, sat on the mat beside this fellow, put one foot in his armpit and one foot on the side of his neck, caught the injured arm, and pulled. It was reset! The recovery was extremely quick. I knew the team, I used to practise there, and this particular man recovered very quickly.

Afterwards, I enquired about it. The chap who did the job was, I think, a surgeon, but in any case some judo men were skilled in something called *soi kotsu* or bone setting. One of the things they said was: *If the joint can be set in a few seconds, there is very little lasting damage, and it will heal very quickly. If it can be set within two hours, then still there will be a relatively quick recovery. If it is more than two hours, however, then it is going to take quite a time.*

This can be applied to a spiritual fall. If we have a bad failure, we generally feel, 'Oh, will I ever be any good?' Or, 'Why do these things happen? Why do I do these things? Why do they do these things?' and so it goes on. Now, if in a few seconds we can perform some kind of spiritual practice, then a disaster leaves almost no impression. But if remorse, repentance, regret, despair, or anger go on longer, it will be much harder to recover.

If I want to hit the table and my fist is only half an inch from it, I cannot generate much force. If I really want to smash the table, I have to take the time to raise my fist high, then I can make a big blow. In the same way, the great obstacles of repentance and remorse, the feeling of failure and despair, take time to mount. If, in those few early seconds, one can quickly get away to a spiritual training practice, then by the time the blow comes down, one is no longer there!

One teacher told us about this sort of fall: *The consequences to your own mind take a little time to mount. When you feel yourself beginning to get angry—it cannot happen immediately, you feel it coming—quickly move before the thing has marshalled its force, so that you are out of the way.*

The instant resetting of the elbow was one vivid example which I saw and it made an impression on me because it was so dramatically effective. Here is another one. This is a poem. It is probably about the thirteenth or fourteenth century from the School of the Spear. The men of the spear especially developed the psychological side because the technique of the spear is very simple; there is very little technical excellence. It is mainly instantaneous response and anticipation; there is no gap between the opponent's move and the response. As today, they used to be arranged in grades. The judo grades are familiar to me— if you are, say, a third black belt and you are going to meet a fourth black belt, well, you are going to lose, aren't you? And the poem says:

To meet a superior in grade—
the only way to go, is completely to forget
that a higher grade is bound to win.

You may say, 'Well, how can you forget that?' But, it can be forgotten. The higher grade—that is all in the past. There is a lot of luck attached to attaining grades, and a lot of luck attached to skills, and a man may be off that day. Completely forget that a higher grade is bound to win. At the present moment, with no grades and no circumstances of any kind, the lower grade is no lower grade.

Similarly, if the higher grade thinks, 'I am bound to win!' that is the way he may lose, because he is not putting out his full alertness. He thinks that the other man is thinking, 'I'm absolutely terrified! I hope he doesn't throw me too hard!' But suppose the lower grade is not terrified . . .

It is much easier to compete with somebody who has practised for a year than with somebody who has never done it at all. You know what he will do. He will do the right things, but he won't be good enough at them. If it is somebody who has never done it at all, however, you have no idea what he will do! Most of it will be absolutely useless, of course, but it may be unexpected—you don't know. With the partly trained opponent, you know what he will do—it won't be good enough and you can handle it all easily.

There is a story which is told all over the East about a merchant who gets drunk on top of a high city wall. He falls off this thirty foot wall to the ground. But he happens to fall on top of another merchant, and kills him. By extraordinary chance he himself is all right. The magistrate is brought in and says, 'Of course it was an accident, but you were drunk and you've got to pay compensation to the sons.'

The lucky merchant says, 'Yes, yes, yes, of course.' And the sum is agreed.

But the two sons say, 'The law says a life for a life. As well as the compensation, this man should give his life. He's killed our father! His life should go.'

The magistrate says, 'Well, it is in the case of murder, that the law says that.'

The sons persist, 'No! A life for a life. Justice!'

The magistrate says, 'Don't you think mercy would be better?'

And they say, 'No! Justice! We're asking for justice.'

Finally the magistrate says, 'Then you will have the exact justice. My officers will put a rope around the man and stand him in that exact place, and the two of you can go on top of the wall and jump on him. The eldest first, and if he misses, the second one.'

Well now, the whole event is absolutely inconceivable, but still it could happen. When you are up against an absolute beginner, he might do things just as risky and crazy, so much so that you do not even consider them—like jumping on you from the top of a wall. The absolute beginner is, therefore, much harder to handle than somebody who knows the rules but isn't too good at them.

The point is, to forget differences of grade in such circumstances and the thought, 'Oh, he is bound to win,' or, 'He is bound to lose.' These are the things which fix the result beforehand, which need not be fixed at all.

In the poems of the School of the Spear, there is a phrase *shinki ki-itsu* which comes very often—*shin* (intention) and *ki* (the initiated movement) *ki-itsu*—coming to one, no gap between them. Normally when I intend to do something, I think, 'Supposing it goes wrong . . ? All right, yes! I'll do it!' There is a gap.

They illustrate this sometimes by saying that your intentions and actions should be like a rope which goes smoothly over a pulley. If the rope has a knot in it, there is a check when it comes to the pulley, and then it jerks. When the knot comes again, there is another check, and it goes on jerkily.

In the same way, when there is a flow of action and suddenly I think, 'How are we doing?' that checks it. Or, when I am working at something and somebody comes and watches me, that checks it.

Well, the point is to undo the knot of that rope, so that it will run freely. There is then no 'I' thinking: *How is it going? Will it come off? Will I get anything for this? Will I be penalized if it goes wrong?* All those things are like knots in a rope. Undo the knot in the meditation and the daily practice.

The teacher says, 'There is rubbish in the mind. There is no free space. The mind is full of rubbish.'

Another teacher says, 'It is not the great passions, it is not the great sins, it is the casual, silly little thoughts which prevent your spiritual progress. Learn to abandon them, to give them up.' It takes energy to hold them—we don't realize that—like carrying a book under the arm. If you carry a book for some time—twenty minutes or so—and if you then trip and fall, you won't let go of the book and take the fall, you will hold onto it. The book has become part of you. In the same way, all sorts of absolutely silly attitudes which we recognize as silly, and which we don't need, are with us, and we're holding them. We're unconscious of it, just as someone becomes unconscious of holding a book under the arm, but if we come to realize—in experience, in meditation especially—that this is an effort, we can let it go. Take it up again, if necessary, and let it go, if necessary. Then the movements will become smoother and easier. And then, he says, 'when your mind is cleared of rubbish, you can play!'

From playing, inspiration and creativity comes—not from the chattering mind. In playing, the rules are given up. It is not a question of deliberately breaking the rules. People often think that if you break the rules, you will be setting yourself free. We may, for example, say, 'Oh, they threw off the restraints of tonal music and they sought for newer and freer methods of expressing their inspiration, beyond the constraints of tonality.' The question is, are these compositions any good? That is the real point—not whether they are new.

Beethoven's pupils thought they were better than Beethoven. They wouldn't play his sonatas in public. Czerny never played Beethoven's sonatas at a concert.

They weren't played in public, in fact, for thirty years or so. Hallé was the first to play the full cycle of sonatas about forty years after Beethoven died. Before that they said that most of them really weren't suitable! Czerny wrote pieces for four pianos, with two pianists at each piano—marvellous! Poor old Beethoven had written for only one piano, and one pianist.

We think that by breaking the rules, or having no rules, we shall get inspiration and freedom: *Don't teach the children by telling them what to do. They need to express their creativity.* Well, this is just getting drunk on words. Enormous assumptions are hidden under this. There is a Chinese phrase which says: *With the untrained, the things of Heaven may take shape within their hearts, but they do not take shape beneath their hands.* There may be inspiration and creativity there—it is arguable that there *always* is—without some technique, however, without some restraints, without some forms, these things of Heaven don't take shape.

Ittokusai

Ittokusai (Yamada Jiro) (1866-1930) was famous as a fencing (*kendo*) master, and as a Buddhist. He had a great influence on the fencing and spiritual atmosphere of the time, especially on lay Zen. A book of his life was printed privately and a copy was given to me by a Zen master, Omori Sogen, who was himself also a fencing master. It is not easily available, and I was reluctant to take it, but he insisted. There was a sort of unspoken understanding that I would translate at least some extracts from it. This book is a compilation of things which were written some eighty or so years ago, so it is in the old Japanese and is fiendishly difficult to read. It was an enormous compliment to be given it from that Zen teacher. The trouble is you have to live up to these compliments, and it took me ages to decipher the first few paragraphs. When you begin to understand the conventions and the context in which it was written, however, then it is not so difficult. This is a translation of the short chapter called 'Character and Conduct: Fragments'.

The master used to say to children, 'Money won't stay with you.' He never said what would stay.

In letters to children he wrote: *Try not to become hoarders.* And again: *Money is something which life deposits with you for a time, so if you have anything over from living your ordinary life in society, use it for the good of society.*

His own preference was for the simplest clothes and food, living in a shack and practising the strictest economy in everything.

His letters to children read as if they were written to a noble family.

With new acquaintances, the master kept his own dignity, but always showed great respect for them.

If, when the master was talking to people, someone said something unworthy or abusive, he always took it and interpreted it in a worthy or refined sense. Often the speaker, becoming ashamed of what he had said, corrected his expression.

The master was very modest. When he heard that disciples who had received from him a letter—brushed in his wonderful brush strokes—were having them mounted and kept as treasures, he took to writing to everyone with a pen instead.

In talking to someone, the master never spoke of any faults of the other. For instance, if in a supporter's party he encountered some noisy vulgar shouter, he would disregard it and say something like, 'In the old days there was one style of giving silent support, wasn't there . . ?' and follow this up with a further topic, so leading the talk in another direction. If a doubt arose about some crucial point, the master used to express his assent by tapping sharply with his fan on his knee.

As to the degree of progress along the Way of training, namely the spiritual state attained, he used to say that if someone had not reached it himself, then however elaborately that person tried to describe it in words, they would be useless. Whereas if someone had himself attained it, then ordinary language would be quite sufficient.

The master treated others with kindly tolerance, but himself with utmost severity. When he was thinking of accepting an offer to become the Kendo Shihan, head teacher, at the famous Shoka University, he went into the mountains at Myogi, performed spiritual practices, and conducted a self-examination as to whether he was inwardly qualified to be a Shihan teacher.

One of his pupils, the late Seki Kozo, during his military career could shout at a soldier with such concentrated energy (*ki*) that the soldier would fall unconscious. When the teacher heard of this incident, he gave a little smile. But when he heard that Seki, in a rough game with children, had again used his *ki-ai* shout to make one fall unconscious, he severely reprimanded him in a voice grown suddenly harsh.

On making a visit to the master, it was never necessary to prepare anything beforehand. Those who went with a burning concern about what to do in the Way always profited immensely from the meeting. It happened again and again that people went and came away without a single word uttered. Sometimes they could not help a rueful smile with the thought that they might as well never have gone. But then they found, to their amazement, that the anxieties or distress that had been filling their hearts when they went, had cleared up, and their hearts were now full of radiance and life.

He said to his pupils, 'When you are reading an exalting book, have the same attitude as when facing a great man.'

One day, when he came out of the training hall after practising with the pupils, he found that someone had tied a big dog to the gatepost, and it was trying to get free. He went straight up to the prisoner and started patting its head. Then the owner came running up, white-faced, calling, 'Master, be careful, be careful!' But seeing that the dog had become perfectly quiet, he choked back his words. It seems that the dog was known to be aggressive and vicious, and it had bitten people who had gone near it.

He often said that however wild an animal might be, if one's own heart is pervaded by the idea of absolute harmlessness, then the animal will do no harm either. Moreover, in front of the teacher, even a raving madman became as gentle and compliant as a pet cat.

Too many to list are the cases where sick people, given up by the doctors, were saved by the master, and still today there are many who believe that he was somehow like a god. At a session of spiritual healing, he and the patient became one. And, in fact, just after the healing, the two pulses were taken, and it was found that the two-pulse beats were in unison.

When the master left the house, he was always on the lookout for books, but he never haggled over the price. Often a bookseller had got something for the master which turned out to be no use for him. Still, he always asked to buy it. As he often said, 'If you don't sometimes get caught into buying a bad book, you won't pick up the rare treasures either.'

He was thus demonstrating the truth of the saying: *There is usefulness even in uselessness.*

He often told us, 'Every night, when I review the past day, from getting up to going to bed, I am really ashamed—full of failures, full of failings.' Up to the day of his death, the master never missed doing this spiritual practice of reflection.

Hanging in the teacher's room was a scroll brushed by Katsu Kaishu himself, which read:

Be sincere and without show;
never try to become great.

The teacher often said that he would like to die while practising kendo, or at any rate, die in the practice hall.

The master was hard on himself, but magnanimous towards others. If, for instance, he was warned by someone against some third party, he would listen to the accusation of wrongdoing, and then say, 'He's just like me, isn't he?' or, 'We are all like that these day...' and would not join in the condemnation on his own account.

When a certain disciple was leaving to go on military service, he asked the master to help him select a sword from the repository to take with him. The master went in and, from his own collection, chose just one. This alone he brought back for him, remarking that the others should not be exposed [to choosing or refusing] but should stay in the repository.

The master was never sparing of formal manners. The Third Middle School converted part of the garden into a kendo practice hall. When he came into the garden to pass into the hall, he always made a bow. Often, coming across students sweeping the ground or cleaning the hall, he paid a similar respect to them.

In middle age, the teacher brushed on a self-portrait the phrase: *Sincere as a clear mirror.* He always kept this carefully with him.

The conversation which the master liked most to take part in was about the art [of kendo swordsmanship]. In a deep, strong voice—level or animated according to the case—he would pursue the subject untiringly. At some of his unexpected illustrations, hearers would find themselves unconsciously drawn to the master, and finally be in complete accord with him. They recognized that what the teacher said was the very essence of kendo. After hearing him even once, they seemed to become different people, not only in their understanding and practise of kendo in the practice hall, but in their daily lives as well.

Like the sun, the teacher gave an energizing life to those who faced him. People felt something like a light—pure, strong, and overflowing with compassion—radiating from the master.

As to health, the master used to say, 'The great *ki*-energy holds in its essence quite enough to nourish the human body. So if one can take in and absorb the breath of *ki*, one will not need other nourishment. Though the ordinary person does not have to try like that, still one must not cease to be aware of the possibility.'

About education in schools, the master said, 'School is a place for creating human beings. It is not for wearying the brains with things that do not really matter, but a one-pointed training to lay down a foundation for the future.'

The master had the greatest reverence for Yamaga Soko and Hirayama Shiryu. One of the Master's treasures was a piece of brushwork by Shiryu. When showing it to children, he said, 'Look at the manly strength of the brush strokes. To make them, there had to be the energy by which the ink swirls up to heaven.' In these words he also indicated the highest peak of kendo.

The master wrote on the Diploma of Proficiency awarded to one of his pupils, the single word: *Infinite (mu-kyuu)*

The master had a very keen intuitive perception of right and wrong, good and bad. But when he thus recognized that one who faced him was a wrongdoer, he never had any expression of dislike, nor did his voice change. In fact, his behaviour became more and more cordial and earnest, as he explained what to do to follow the Way.

A week before the master died, his disciple Onishi got him to allow a photograph. It was taken in the garden, standing facing East, his hands quietly folded, enjoying the sunshine. His countenance was like a clear crystal, without a trace of passion or ambition. As he stood there, caressed by the kindly warmth of a gentle springlike breeze, the watchers felt there was a shining godlike light radiating from his whole frame. When the master himself saw the developed print, he said, 'This is the first time I have come out in a photograph looking really human.'

These are about half of the fragments which were collected, and I think it gives some sort of picture of the teacher, Ittokusai, even in these very short extracts. There are others. When he wrote to children, for instance, he wrote as if he was writing to the nobility.

Some of them have a great charm of humility and modesty, yet he was one of the master swordsmen of the time. So he had both 'the death-dealing sword' and 'the life-giving sword', and we can see that beyond the sword, which normally is a weapon that can kill, there was the swordless, which gives life.

There were those who practised austerities, and one of the austerities described—which the kendo men practised—was this *ki-ai* shout. The effects were real. They were practised by people whose lives depended on them. But one man who was an expert in this told me that in the end it is a frustration, that the range is very limited, and in fact it does no good to anybody. The master strongly reprimanded Seki for showing off with this ability, especially in front of children.

I have taken part in a test of one of these things and the range was very, very small. The effect was real, but it led to no good. One teacher described it as fireworks. He said, 'With fireworks you go, "Ooh..!" But you can't warm your hands with fireworks, and you cannot write a letter by the light of them—they are absolutely useless, except to amaze. And furthermore,' he said, 'there is an inherent, latent contradiction at the very heart of these things.' He left that for us to ponder over.

Like That

In Chinese calligraphy as it developed to heights undreamed of in the West, there were three main styles: The Formal Style, the Running Style, described as waving grasses and running streams, and the ultimate loosening called the Grass Style, described in terms of Soaring Phoenixes and Fighting Dragons.

This last style was highly developed in Japan, and especially by Zen masters. They used it to express experienced spiritual truth, not merely by the words but by the very brushwork itself.

The accompanying poem is:

LIKE THAT

As in spring, the flowers,
As in autumn, the moon.

In Japanese aesthetics, the Three Beautiful Things are:
Tsuki, the moon; Yuki, snow; and Hana, flowers.

Only in the extended list do wine, women and song
appear. The Five Beautiful Things are Tsuki, Yuki,
Hana, and then Iro, colour, implying also love-making,
and Sake, rice-wine (which has however a low alcohol
content).

The great character on the right of the picture
means 'Like That', or 'Thus'. It means: 'That is the
way things are; do not expect them to be different.'

But this does not mean apathy. In spring, to look
at the flowers and appreciate their beauty without
wanting to appropriate them; in autumn, not to waste
thought by longing for flowers, but to appreciate the
wonder of the moon in the clear skies. Flowers, however beautiful, have a sadness about them because they
will fade and fall, but the moon does not pass away.
There is a meaning for the whole of life: in spring-
time, to realize that the flowers will pass, and enjoy
them without trying to capture or appropriate them
for selfish ends, and then when autumn comes, to turn
to contemplation of the calmness which is ever within.

In India, the Supreme Self is represented by the
symbol of the sun, but in the Far East, it is often the

full moon. In the second half of life, attention is to move from the short-range relations with the flowers upwards to the heavens, as the skies are cleared of personal selfish pettiness, a calm radiance takes over from the little anxiety-flashes of the small world.

The calligrapher is Ji-un, who was a follower not only of Zen but also of the philosophical Tendai sect, the Shingon mantra sect, and originally the ancient Indian Vinaya, in whose temples some of the early Zen masters resided before the establishment of specifically Zen temples.

Sword and Mind

Ittokusai had a big influence in reviving the spiritual elements in the traditional training of the samurai in Japan. Zen Buddhism had played a great part in that spiritualization, much as chivalry had in the West. The latter succeeded partially in refining and ennobling people who were originally little more than gangsters. In Japan, similarly, the cult of force, the naked sword, was partially spiritualized by the efforts of a chain of masters of the so-called knightly arts— including what became judo—and by Zen teachers at Kamakura and elsewhere who influenced them.

The so-called feudal Japan was not so very long ago. Fairly recently, there was a very senior Member of the Japanese Diet whose grandfather had committed hara-kiri because he had displeased the head of his clan. That was about 1860. So the memories were still alive. After the Meiji Restoration of that period, many of the samurai were suddenly out of a job. They had been the administrators of the country, and some of them were now very dangerous people. I give one little example, which was, I believe, translated into English in A.B. Mitford's *Tales of Old Japan*.

In those days, and even later in the century, it was a terrible insult if a samurai's scabbard was touched by anyone in passing. So a samurai who was orderly and did not want a fight kept his scabbard close to his side in the street. On one occasion, according to a newspaper report, a rather poorly dressed samurai passed three others who had been drinking. They turned on him and claimed that his scabbard had touched one of theirs. He denied it, and even offered to apologise for any supposed insult. But they refused. 'You have insulted us,' they said. 'You've got to pay for it.' So the three of them lined up, facing this single man. There were bystanders, but no one ventured to interfere. The newspaper report says that the single swordsman advanced steadily towards the central opponent. The man on his right thought he saw an opportunity and made a cut at his head. There was a lightning counterattack, and he went down bathed in blood. Then the opponent on the left came on, and he too was instantly cut down. The third man ran away. The lone samurai wiped his sword, and then went to report the matter to the local police, as the law required.

I have presented this account because Ittokusai, when talking about the practice of kendo in his time with bamboo swords in a training hall, said, 'It is no longer a question of life and death, and so the spirit of intensity has been lost.' Of course, he was not recommending that kendo men should practise with real swords. He meant that when you know that nothing serious can really happen, you may easily lose the spirit of kendo. The whole intensity is lost if you think that, after all, the worst will be a hit on the head with a bamboo sword. He added that if you practise like this, it is of no value for life.

We can see in our own time that tennis or golf is of little value for life if it is just getting skill in hitting a ball with precision and force. There may be some value in it if it is practised in the spirit of sport—which many so-called sportsmen fail to understand. To be able to keep your temper when losing, and refrain from exulting when you win, is a training in independence, and an advantage in life. But the spirit of kendo ought to give much more than that.

Notice in the following extract how Ittokusai not only explains technique, but also how he speaks of something much higher than that:

This dharma of the sword is made up of two elements: *Ri* (inspiration) and technique. Technique follows the nature of the form of the sword. When the adaptive movements of the body have been learned, one has to learn how to base them on *ri*. Then a natural inspiration appears, which develops into an understanding of the states called 'emptiness' and 'fullness', which are the, as yet, unmanifest signs of winning or losing. Broadly speaking, technique is easy to practise because it has a form. This is especially true when in kendo the opponents come face to face armed merely with bamboo swords. In that case, all idea of danger, of life and death depending on this single combat, is lost. One sees, then, how the great enemies of wrong thinking and delusive ideas make a sudden attack on the brightness of heart and body, so that the living freedom of movement is lost. Thoughts of self-advantage spring up. Tricks and stratagems are devised. Or again, one falls into fixed patterns of sword technique to defend oneself. All these come bubbling up in one's breast, so that in the end the spiritual blaze of energy becomes feeble and slight, and in fact is destroyed. It degenerates into hesitation, evasion, and finally fear. One can no longer understand clearly either one's opponent or oneself. One misses one's own opportunities of besting the opponent, and is, on the contrary, pathetically open to that opponent's attack. This is why in kendo one must absolutely cut away all thoughts about winning, and become aware of whether one's spirit can meet the opponent's cut and thrust without flinching, or whether it cannot. One must practise going deeper and deeper into this.

You will notice that there are phrases which seem to be absurd. *To give up all idea of winning*, for example. Before looking at this, I will make a few general remarks. First of all, there is the word *ri*. In normal use it means something like 'a principle'. However, in the West words like 'principle' have very strong intellectual associations. There is the *principle* of double entry in accounting, and the *principle* of first in, first out (FIFO) in storekeeping. The principle of FIFO is that the goods which the store takes in first, should be the first to go out. If FIFO is not followed, the goods taken in first go to the back of the store, remain there and finally become useless. These principles are abstract ideas. They have practical use, but they are no more than ideas; they are not experiences. *Ri*, in the kendo texts and in Zen, is not simply an idea. I have here translated *ri* as 'inspiration', which means an in-breath of new life. A principle is not usually a living thing, but *ri* is a living experience.

Consider this phrase: *The right hand should hold the sword lightly but firmly.* What does it mean? If you hold it lightly, it will wobble about. If you hold it firmly to prevent the wobble, then it will not be held lightly. The second part seems to contradict the first. In the end you don't know what to do.

In an ancient Asian city, one passed under three arches as one came to the king's palace at the centre. On the first arch was written in big letters: **BE BOLD.** Passing under that and riding on, one came to the second arch. On this was written in big letters: **BE BOLD.** Passing on still further, one came to the third arch on which was written: **BUT NOT TOO BOLD.** Here, too, the last advice cancels out the earlier ones. It can be the same with texts on the inner training. If readers don't have a background of practise, they feel they've got something, but then on reading a bit further, it is all taken away again.

Now, a new subject about how to practise movement. Suppose, in the West, we are being taught in our physical exercises to stretch out the arms to the sides. We stretch them. 'No,' yells the instructor, 'stretch more fully!' We stretch more fully and that is accepted. But in the Far East, a teacher will say, 'Now feel you are putting your fingers through the walls.' We try it, but somehow find it unpleasant; we're afraid our fingertips will get bruised, and we hold back a little. The teacher sees this at once, and calls out, 'No, through the walls, right through!' After a few attempts, we begin to get the feeling, and then as our fingers GO through the walls, we feel the shoulders and arms s-t-r-e-t-c-h. They stretch much more than they would do by just trying to push them out. The clear visualization is the secret. A bare effort of will is not so effective.

To return to holding the sword with the right hand 'lightly but firmly', what is the clear visualization for that? Ittokusai tells us to imagine that we see a baby chick just breaking free from its shell. We want to help it, so we have to hold it very delicately, and yet firmly. And he says, 'Think of that as the example for the right hand.'

It is extremely useful to know about this method of teaching and learning. Dr Kano dismissed much of

Western physical exercises as 'dead movement', because they lack this kind of picture. Dead exercises may build muscles, but they do nothing to improve co-ordination and precision. They have no purposeful picture with them. The Eastern method helps to train the mental side as well as the physical.

Now Ittokusai's teachings contain a certain amount of technical instruction in the field of kendo, but there is no need to explain that here. What is interesting is that he speaks of something higher than correct technique. He will say, for instance, 'that when mind and vital energy are united in emptiness, right action takes place of itself, independently. 'It is,' he says, 'as if a god acted through YOU.'

Someone may object, 'Oh, he can't use words like that. It doesn't mean anything. He calls himself a Buddhist, so he's not supposed to believe in gods . . .' Well, he uses such words because that is what it feels like.

One point is to get people to practise and find out for themselves what it is like. A second point is that such words may help a student to recognize something that has happened. At first these things often happen just for a moment, and then the inspiration passes; a wonder has happened, but it slips by, almost unnoticed. The man thinks, 'Oh, that went well. He seemed to walk into it just as I moved. I wasn't thinking of trying anything, I just moved, and he got caught. Lucky, I suppose.' Here is a brief quote:

The Song of the Ri
When he strikes,
Let him not think that he makes the strike.
Let the strike be no strike,
the cut, no cut. To strike is to lose.
Not to strike is to win.

The distinction between *ri* (inspiration), and the techniques of kendo done with a bamboo sword, is clear from this verse. Generally these days, the fashion is to practise kendo techniques on their own, without regard for posture, or for unification of mind and vital energy, and so on. The practitioners prize only skill and speed in the action of the sword. Cleverness in these gets highly praised. But it is all a degeneration, which arises from constant practise with the bamboo sword, and it misses the central point of kendo. These things are merely branches and leaves of kendo; they are far away from its deep root. In such a case, though one may think one has sufficient to meet a crisis, in fact, one has not.

Conscious actions, though practised repeatedly till they are expert, are not inspiration which is the innermost truth of kendo. What is meant by this inspiration? There have been some who believed that it is simply what is called 'conditioned reflexes'. They give the example of learning to drive a car. First of all, you are intensely conscious of each separate action as you learn it, and then, gradually, the individual actions drop out of awareness; they become conditioned reflexes. It is thought that as the driving becomes more and more a matter of reflexes, it becomes better. It is automatic, as they say.

In fact, people do not become better and better at driving their cars. Unless they consciously practise, they become more and more sloppy. They get worse, though they may get more skilful at a bad method.

In the same way, golfers take lessons at the beginning and reach a certain standard. After that they no longer have lessons, but just play. They may develop a bad swing. True, they may get more skilful at using this bad swing. Sometimes you see rather good results from a very poor swing. But if these golfers have to play when they are a bit tired, or have bad colds, often their swing will fall to pieces completely; they can't do anything at all. Whereas, one who has continued to take lessons, and so has corrected bad habits before they became fixed, will still play reasonably well even when tired.

The writer Arthur Koestler was a clever man, but he had no idea of anything beyond technique. He heard of the state of kendo and Zen where an action takes place without any conscious decision, and believed this must be a conditioned reflex. His explanation, therefore, was: *One who has practised kendo continuously for a long time will acquire these reflex actions; they will take place without his intention.*

Koestler thought the movements would be automatic, like an experienced driver automatically braking when a child runs across the road. But this idea is quite wrong. Why? Because reflex action merely produces what has been repeatedly done before. There is nothing new in it. And, in fact, in judo and kendo, one can control such an opponent through his reflexes. If I do this, he will do that automatically, every time.

We do not know what a kendo master, or a true master at anything, will do. It is a fresh inspiration each time. The difference between *ri* and the conditioned reflex is this: In the reflex situation, the mind is not thinking about this automatic action, but mind is not clear either; it is full of other thoughts. As Ittokusai says, 'In a contest, minds are seething with ideas of: *How can I win? Shall I try that? Suppose he has a counter?* and so on. Because the mind is not clear, there is no inspiration.'

The mind has to be without thought. The word *ri* literally means 'without mind', but to us that could mean something inert. Perhaps 'without minding' would be a better attempt at translation. There is calm awareness with no ripples in it. With the car-driving reflexes, it is true that I am not thinking about the particular movements, but I am thinking about many other things. 'Those other things,' adds Ittokusai, 'are all about my self-advantage, what I will do if I win, and how bad it will be if I lose.'

For inspiration, there must be no purposes in the

mind. We can note here that this is a very ancient theme in the Far East. In the ancient Chinese classic Chuang Tze, there is a little section which runs something like this:

> The Yellow Emperor went on a pleasure trip. He climbed the great mountain and surveyed the Red Plain. He returned, and found that he had lost his black pearl. So he sent Knowledge-by-Reasoning to find it, but Reasoning could not find it. Then he sent Keen-Eyed to find it, but Keen-Eyed could not find it. Then he sent Big Words to find it, but Big Words could not find it. Then he employed Purposeless. And Purposeless found it. 'Strange,' said the great Emperor, 'that Purposeless should have been the one to find it!'

The interpretation of the Chinese characters is quite involved, but 'Purposeless' is from the meaning 'no symbol', 'no form'. The second element of the character is literally an elephant, and the tradition is that the Chinese came across the bones of an elephant before they had ever seen one. They pieced together the bones and tried to construct the form of an elephant; hence the character for elephant came also to mean an abstract form, or a symbol. One point of the story is that inspiration will flash only when mind is cleared of laying traps and clever counters, and winning and losing generally. It is Purposeless who finds the black pearl of inspiration.

How is this state to be reached? By inner practices. One of them, which kendo men do, or used to, is the following. You might like to try it yourself.

Sit reasonably upright, the head balanced on the spine. Feel that you are on a hilltop, facing the blue sky. Feel that in your lap you have a cloth filled with pebbles. You sit there, and a thought comes up in your mind. Mentally pick up a pebble and throw it with the thought, away down the hill— *not wanted.* Another thought comes up: *That quarrel I had yesterday, I could have said . . .* Throw it away with a pebble. Another thought: *What am I going to do about . . ?* Throw it away—*not wanted.* Another thought . . . Chuck it away in the same manner.

Well, if you go on doing this, finally thoughts become less. They cannot exist without your support. You sit and chuck them away with the pebbles. There is a sort of satisfaction as the thought and pebble go rolling away down the hill. Then, just sit under the blue sky with no more thoughts coming up. Try it now for a few minutes.

Jottings from Zen Master Bukko

Bukko (Buddha-Light) was an honorific title bestowed posthumously by the Japanese Emperor on a Chinese monk, Tsu Yuen, one of the thirteenth-century Buddhist teachers who brought Zen to Japan.

From childhood, Bukko had a fondness for temples and Buddhism. One day he heard a monk recite two lines from a famous Taoist classic:

> *The shadow of the bamboo sweeps the steps,*
>   *but the dust does not stir;*
> *The moon's disc bores into the lake,*
>   *but the water shows no scar.*

This inspired him to search, and finally he found a teacher who set him the koan riddle: *No Buddha-nature in a dog.* It took him six years to pass this one. He could now sit in meditation for long periods without tiring. Sometimes he passed into trance where breath stops. He said that the inner state was that of a bird escaping from a cage. After this, when he closed his eyes he saw nothing but vast space, and when he opened them he saw everything in this vastness. The teacher still did not confirm this as final but gave him another koan. He passed this second one under the teacher's successor, who gave him a full confirmation.

Later, when the Mongols were sweeping over China, they entered the temple where he was staying. The others ran, but Bukko calmly remained sitting. A Mongol soldier came up with drawn sword. Bukko recited a poem:

> *In heaven and earth, no crack to hide in;*
> *Joy to know the man is void and things too*
>   *are void!*
> *Splendid the great Mongolian Longsword—*
> *The lightning flash cuts the spring breeze.*

The Mongols were impressed with his courage, and left him alone.

Zen was being introduced into Japan during the whole thirteenth century. Bukko went to Japan in 1280 and lived there for the remaining six years of his life. He was one of the great Chinese priests who brought Zen to Kamakura, the *de facto* capital. The country faced the imminent threat of the Mongols, who had conquered a good deal of the known world, including much of China. Towards the end of the century,

Kublai Khan launched two invasions which were re-
pulsed under the leadership of Tokimune the Regent,
one of Bukko's best pupils. He is regarded as a sort of
bodhisattva whose genius saved Japan, aided by
favourable winds like those which saved Britain from
the Armada. In those times of national crisis, the role
of the warrior was paramount, and Zen inspired the
warriors. They, in turn, affected Zen, which in Japan
took on a strong tradition of warrior virtues. Some of
Bukko's Zen interviews are given in *The Warrior
Koans* collection. (See my *The Warrior Koans: Early
Zen in Japan.*)

In his six years in Japan, Bukko never learned much
Japanese, so his sermons and addresses to Kamakura
audiences were given in Chinese. They were translated
into Japanese by a priest whose name is pronounced
Gi-o in Japanese, and who came from the same district
in China as Bukko, so could understand his dialect.
The exposition is not on Indian lines of logical exposition, but follows the Zen method as it had developed
in China. To put it bluntly, both Indians and Chinese
like to quote, but Indians generally understand what
they quote, at least intellectually. The Chinese tended
to quote without necessarily understanding. Perhaps
it was to get round this that the genius of the Chinese
masters developed a system of giving riddling phrases,
to which it is impossible to find a solution in the scriptures. If a teacher says: *Two hands brought together
make a clap. What is the sound of one hand?* It is
difficult to find a quotation to answer this. But the

master insists on an answer. If the search is continued, it leads to an experience, and everyone who does it comes to the same experience. In a sense, it is a departure from the logical basis of Buddhism, as some scholars and also priests have pointed out.

There was another transmission of Zen to Kyoto, the formal capital, remote from the soldiers of Kamakura. In Kyoto, Zen developed on more logical lines, based on scriptural texts, whereas in Kamakura, where Bukko and others taught so successfully, it came to be based more and more on pure experience. The *Shonankattoroku* text gives a hundred of the Kamakura interviews, and it is clear that the masters were inventing new riddles based on actual life situations. There were riddles about the moon's reflection in a bucket of water, about a loincloth, about an earthquake, and so on. Some of the answers had to be lived through in the presence of the teacher. Because of the limitations of Bukko's Japanese, his presentation of the riddle had to be short, and the answer, too, had to be short.

Even after he and the other Chinese priests had died and left Japanese successors, the tradition remained that both riddles and answers should continue to be short. In a way, this is typical of Japanese adoption of something foreign. The pupils are not sure which parts of the tradition are essential and which are not. So they are afraid to change anything, lest something essential be lost.

Soon after Bukko died, the tradition was established at the great temples that the answer to the warrior koan should be just a single word. And sometimes this word was just a great shout of fearlessness and defiance of anything the world could do. When the news came that the first Mongol invasion fleet had been sighted, Tokimune sought an interview with Bukko, which ended in a great shout. It was said to have frightened the deer in a cave, which is in fact a good hundred yards from the interview room. The shout had to be given from a state in which the shouter is ready to jump over a cliff. The interview gave the warriors freedom from the fear of death.

However, after the Mongol invasions had been repelled, and the Japanese equivalent of the Wars of the Roses had finally subsided, fearlessness was not the only thing required of the ruling class. After 300 years, Kamakura Zen had narrowed to a single track, and the succession died out. No new Bukko arose to revive it, and a new succession of teachers was established from among the followers of Hakuin, whose Zen embraced all areas of life.

An Outline of Bukko's Teachings

What follows is a brief note of some of Bukko's main teachings as given in the *Record of Bukko*— the brief sermons preached by him in Japan and then circulated among his mainly warrior disciples at Enkakuji temple in Kamakura. They are hard to follow in isolation, so first a sort of outline of the teachings is given as a rough framework, then a very free rendering of a few of them as they stand, each supplemented with others taken from elsewhere in the *Bukko Goroku, The Sayings of Bukko,* and occasionally a few extra comments.

The way out of life and death is not some special technique; the essential thing is to penetrate to the root of life and death. It is in the centre of everyone, and everything else is dependent on it. Zen is to pierce through to it.

Zen sitting is not some sort of operation to be performed. It is going into one's true original nature before father or mother were born. The self seeks to grasp the self, but it is already the self, so why should it go to grasp the self? Look into it. Where was it then? Where is it now? When life ends, where does it go? When you feel you cannot look any more, look and see how that inability to look appears and disappears. As you look and see how the looking arises and goes, *satori*, realization, will arise of itself.

At the beginning you have to take up a koan riddle. One such is this: *What is your true face before father and mother were born.* For one facing the turbulence of life and death, such a koan clears away the sandy soil and opens up the golden treasure which was there from the beginning, the ageless root of all things.

In concentration on a koan, there is a time of rousing the spirit of inquiry, a time of breaking clinging attachments, a time of furious dashing forward, and there is a time of damping the fuel and stopping the boiling. In general, meditation has to be done with urgency, but if after three or five years the urgency is still maintained by force, the tension becomes a wrong one and it is a serious condition. Many lose heart and give up. In such a case, the koan is to be thrown down. Then there is a cooling. The point is that many people come to success if they first have the experience of wrestling with a koan and later reduce the effort, but few come to success when they are putting out exceptional effort. After a good time, the rush of thoughts outward and inward, subsides naturally, and the true face shows itself as the solution to the koan. And mind, free from all motivations, always appears as void and absolute sameness, shining like the brightness of heaven, at the centre of the vast expanse of phenomenal things, and needing no polishing or cleaning. This is beyond all concepts, beyond being and nonbeing.

Leave your innumerable knowing and seeings and understandings, and go to that greatness of space.

When you come to that vastness, there is no speck of Buddhism in your heart, and then you will have the true sight of the buddhas and patriarchs. The true nature is like the immensity of space, which contains all things. When you can conform to high and low, square and round, to all regions equally, that is it. The emptiness of the sea lets waves rise, the emptiness of the mountain valley makes the voice echo, the emptiness of the heart makes the Buddha. When you empty the heart, things appear as in a mirror, shining there without differences in them: *Life and death is an illusion, and all the buddhas one's own body.*

Jottings from the Sayings of Bukko

1. If you live on the heights, on top of the mountain, you are in constant anxiety. You have to hold onto everything in case it falls and is lost to you; your name, your reputation, your status, your money, your learning—you have to look after them, you have to hold onto them all. Otherwise, a moment's carelessness, and one of them will slip down and go on falling right to the bottom of the mountain. And you yourself may fall down too.

It is better to be at the bottom of the mountain already. And if you can remain pure, you will be like a hollow at the mountain foot, which will keep the pure rain and become a little lake. In that lake fish can live in purity and humility at the bottom of the mountain. Keep pure and nourish the fish.

2. A teacher of one of the philosophical schools of Buddhism, a very learned man, said to Bukko, 'I know the holy texts. How is it that I do not have this freedom of realization?' Bukko replied, 'The seeds have been planted; the seeds are there, but the ground is in such a state that they do not strike, they do not germinate. You must dig up all your prejudices and clear the ground of your fixed ideas, and then the seeds will germinate.'

3. In another little sermon Bukko says, 'All of you are sideways on, standing there in the gateway of the temple. You cannot make up your minds whether to come in and really practise for realization. On the other hand, neither can you tear yourselves away and go into the world. You stand there sideways on, half facing in, and half facing away.

Then he added, 'And you have to practise in the right way. There are fish in the sea, but you don't get them by jumping into a boat and going after them with a sword!'

4. The great universe has no outside. The great perfection has no inside. The sea, the moon, the mountain, the cloud, face and delimit each other. Last night the wind changed from east to north, but the great Void has no directions.

Bukko often uses the expression 'the wind changed'.

We are not to curse and complain that the wind changed. People may be fawning on you, and then come to hate you. Someone is a bitter enemy, and then abruptly becomes rather friendly, and you find yourselves working together. A reputation is high, and within half an hour it is lost. A man who has been ignored and despised, a woman who has been slighted, are recognized as great figures. We tend simply to hang on to this and that, but you cannot hang on, the wind changes. So, accept the changes of the wind. In the great Void, there are no directions, no north or south, no east or west, no high or low.

5. You are like starving people who do get some food, put it in their mouths, but then spit it out at once. You are spiritually starving! You hear the great teachings, take them, and then you too spit them out. You don't chew them, you don't digest them, and so they do you no good. Here you are listening to me, but in the next half-hour you will go away, and you will be talking all sorts of nonsense. That means you are spitting out what you had taken in, and it has done you no good at all. There are so many teachers, so many teachings, but immediately afterwards you leave them, and so they do you no good, and give you no life.

6. How can I tell you? The ancients themselves said they did not know, but now you come and ask me to

explain. You want me to cut up the waters with a sword.

One knot and everything is knotted. One loosening and everything is loosened.

Everything is freed, freed from the illness of being Buddha, freed from the illness of being a patriarch, freed from the illness of being a living being in *samsara*. All are already free!

After this sermon, Bukko was asked, 'In that case, what are you doing giving these sermons? If all are already free, there is nothing to be done.'

He replied, 'With a deaf person, you show the gate by pointing. With a blind person you show the gate by knocking on it.'

7. People say: *We have been in ignorance for so long, with so many associations, how can it all be cleared away quickly, in a single lifetime, as the Zen people claim?*

Bukko said, 'The throat may have been very dry, absolutely parched, for a long time, but one good drink of water, and everything is all right.'

8. The Absolute beats the drum.

[The Absolute is a translation of two Chinese characters, read in Japanese as *Shinnyo*. It means 'what it is really like'.]

The *Shinnyo* beats the drum and in India the baby Buddha is formed, and in us the intelligence quickens and becomes bright, and the clouds clear away from the mountain peak. Listen for the throb of infinity: *The Absolute beats the drum.* Listen for that!

9. On the anniversary of Buddha's *nirvana*, Bukko stood up in front of the assembly, pulled in his hands, and rubbed his chest. Then he said, 'The Absolute had a pain in the chest, but rubbed it and everything was all right again.'

10. Bukko banged his staff on the pillar of the meditation hall and said, 'Invest your spiritual energy here, as a merchant invests his money in a new warehouse.'

11. Bukko quoted an incident concerning an old Chinese master: A monk said, 'I cannot manage to realize my true nature. Have you got some means for someone like me?'

The master said, 'I have got no earmuffs on my ears.'

The monk said, 'I can see that for myself.'

The teacher said, 'I have created a mistake.'

The monk said, 'What mistake?'

The teacher said, 'I made you see for yourself something that is not there!'

Bukko set this as a riddle to be solved by his audience.

12. Bukko said, 'It is like the dragon playing with the wisdom-ball. He does not always stay above in absolute transcendence, but plays with it, sometimes letting it drop. But he never lets it fall onto the earth as absolutely real. He plays with it between the two, sometimes tossing it high, and sometimes letting it fall low.'

[The heavenly dragon represents transcendence. He carries a crystal ball of wisdom.]

13. The master whirled his staff around, and then he said, 'If I wave it around, you think, "Ah, but the true nature of the staff is to be still." Then, if I do keep it still, you keep wondering when I'm going to do something with it.'

Then he put out his tongue. He said, 'If I say something, you say, "Ah, but the truth is really silent." And then if I keep my mouth shut, you begin to invent teachings for yourselves!'

14. The great changes take place in the universe, and they are right and perfect as they are. It is our passions, our clinging, that lead to all the suffering and produce all the obstacles.

Bukko points to these things in many different ways. Indians would never stand for the contradictions, but in the Chinese Zen tradition this is how it developed. They are like striking flint and steel to produce a flash of insight, as actual experience. And if one doesn't work, then another one is presented, until one does. Then you have to nurture the glowing tinder and bring it up. For instance, Bukko describes a picture of Bodhidharma sitting in meditation: *It is a dragon coiled up!* Then on another occasion he will say: *Things are perfect as they are. Old Bodhidharma missed the point, coming all that way, first to Sri Lanka and then to China, and standing there banging away at the gate!*

When one comes across such passages, one thinks, 'How was that again?' We feel there is something there, and we think and think. 'Things are perfect as they are. So why change them? Why does Bukko give sermons if things are already perfect?'

Buddhism can be looked at in terms of music, whereas the Vedanta of the Upanishads could correspond to architecture where reality is something immense and unchanging with events, including human events, passing in and out, to and fro, like shadows. They pass away. But the great reality remains, unchanging. In Buddhism, on the other hand, Buddha-nature *is* change. In this sense, Buddhism can be compared to music, the essence of which is also change.

As an example, take the familiar opening chords in Rachmaninov's popular Second Piano Concerto. The movement begins with seven crashing chords.

Most pianists have to fake them today, as Rachmaninov wrote for his own hands, which were exceptional in their stretch. This is a famous dramatic passage. Each chord is different, but there is a dramatic inevitability in the sequence. Listening to it, each one is perfect in itself, but though it is perfect, we do not feel: *Oh, let it stay. It is perfect. Let it stay forever.* The next chord, too, is perfect and the next one. As we listen, we find that the sequence of the chords, too, is perfect. Bukko is saying: *Each chord is perfect, and the sequence is perfect. But you spoil it because when one is being played, you're thinking it should stay. Or else you're thinking of the next one, or perhaps of the last one, or perhaps all these things together. So you don't appreciate the things as they stand.*

The warrior koan collection of 101 Zen interviews *(Shonankattoroku)*, contains ten connected with Bukko. A famous one was this:

A nun-disciple was carrying a lacquer bucket of water for the flowers, and caught sight of the moon reflected in it. She had an intuitive flash, and made a poem:

Carrying the bucket,
I saw the moon reflected in it
When it was held steady.

Her realization was that when the passions are

stilled in the mind, the truth is reflected in it, if only it is held steady. She presented this poem to Bukko, and he said, 'Nun, take the *Heart Sutra* and Go!' Well, you may have read the *Heart Sutra* of some 250 Chinese characters. Perhaps you have a solution, but she went away and did not find one in spite of her efforts. Then, one day, she again brought the lacquer bucket for the flowers, and the bottom fell out of it. She then had a flash of much deeper realization, and presented another poem to the teacher:

The bottom fell out of the bucket!
Now there is no water,
And no moon reflected in it.

The teacher accepted this. She later became a great teacher herself at the nunnery at Tokei—a beautiful temple which still exists.

The *Shonankattoroku* text has one or two cases where Bukko and his great predecessor, Daikaku, are paired in an interesting way. For instance, the importance of the *Heart Sutra* of 250 characters has just been mentioned. A follower of the Lotus sect came to Daikaku and said, 'Your *Heart Sutra* text is too long. Our Lotus invocation—*Reverence to the lotus*—is only seven syllables, and much more suited to the people

As One, receive it.

of today.' Daikaku laughed and said, 'Oh, seven syllables is much too long. If you want to recite a Zen sutra, do it in one word. Now, what is that word?' Afterwards, he set this as a riddle for his disciples. All kinds of attempts were made—*Buddha, heart, sincerity* and others—but Daikaku never approved any. He died without giving the answer. So some of his disciples approached Bukko, his spiritual successor at Kamakura, in the hope of getting an answer. Bukko said, 'Our school is a transmission from heart to heart, and does not need to set up words. If you grasp it, your whole life will be a sutra, and your death will be a sutra. You need no other sutra.'

So here the one-word sutra of Daikaku at Kenchoji is contrasted with the no-word sutra of Bukko at Enkakuji.

A substantial history of Kenchoji has recently been published in Japan, and the author sent me a copy. The Kenchoji records, though much has been lost in a great fire, contain a number of such references to Bukko.

He had women disciples. It is one of the features of Zen that there was no prejudice against women, as there was in some sects. It was sometimes supposed that women intellectually, and in some other ways, were inferior, but this was because they were not educated. In earliest times in India, however, women were respected in religious circles. In one of the oldest Upanishads (about 500 BCE) Maitreyi and Gargi play prominent parts. And there is no indication that this was unusual. In a still earlier Brahmana text, Gargi is called 'the teacher'. But later in India, and in China, women were not educated. In China, to get an education, some girls disguised themselves as boys in order to go to school. But Bodhidharma, the founder of Zen in China, had a woman among his four disciples, and in the *Shonankattoroku* text there are a number of pieces centred on women of the warrior class.

The warrior disciples at Kamakura did not, of course, become monks, but they became what was called *nyudo* (one who has entered the Way). They shaved their heads and took certain vows. Their Zen was layman's Zen of the Rinzai line, which today stresses practice with a series of classical koan riddles. These were based on incidents in early Zen, from the Buddha onwards through the Indian and Chinese patriarchs. In Kamakura warrior Zen, the riddles were incidents that happened in everyday life here and now. It was called *shikin* Zen, or on-the-spot Zen. They are concerned with things like a bucket of water, a teacup, a misreading of a Chinese character, prayers for rain, various popular beliefs and even superstitions.

Some teachers today believe that the present era is suited to this kind of on-the-spot Zen. The form of the answers to the classical riddles leak out. A good teacher will never pass a mere outward imitation, but it can happen—and did happen in Japan—that a particular riddle has an answer in a particular form, and if that form of answer is given, it will be passed. When this happens, Zen decays, as the Rinzai line did in Japan, until Hakuin revived it. The *shikin,* on-the-spot, Zen riddles are living on the first occasion, but since they concern everyday events, they need not harden into lifeless forms.

Traditionally in China, the Zen monasteries and training centres were on the top of mountains, remote from city life. Bukko himself when he was thirteen climbed up to the monastery on a mountain. In these isolated places they became expert in formal meditation sitting. He was given his first koan at seventeen. It took him several years to pass. But in these times, some teachers say, the busy modern laypeople cannot keep at it that long, so they are passed through more easily. It takes many different riddles, however, to keep them from giving up. The chief monasteries in Japan, though often near or in cities, are still called mountain temples. Those who go there are not expected to enter the trance states described of Bukko, where the breathing practically stops. The phenomenon has been studied in India by medical teams; the pulse becomes almost imperceptible. The trance pursued as an end in itself, however, is no guarantee of spiritual growth. Some performers are, frankly, doing it for money. Bukko does not treat it as anything but an occasional by-product of prolonged Zen sitting. Bukko took one more koan, and completed his realization after passing through just two. It took twenty years of intense practice in his case.

If You're Going to Die, Die Quick!

A Japanese woman practised Zen at the beginning of the twentieth century. Her daughter told me about it. The mother was diagnosed as having a serious illness, and the medical science of the time gave her only a few months to live. When she was told, she went to see her Zen teacher in Yokohama. When he heard about it, he just remarked, 'Well, you may be missed for up to three years after your death, but after that no one will remember you at all.' She was taken aback, and pleaded, 'I'm going to die. Can't you help me?' He jumped up, took her by the shoulders and pushed her out the door. 'If you're going to die, die quick!' he said, and slammed the sliding doors together behind her.

She went into one of the little caves in the small cliff at Yokohama, and stayed there to meditate and die quick. On the third night, however, she had a vision of *bodhisattvas* filling the sky, and felt something turn over inside her. She came out and resumed her life, becoming a well-known local figure in Zen, and living into her eighties.

This does seem very harsh, and probably the teacher would not have said this to someone of less strength of character. I can also say that in times of real crisis I have found this phrase a big help: *If you're going to die, die quick!*

Such things are part of a living instruction. It is not a question of always shouting. Some of us need shouts, perhaps at particular times, and there are others who don't need them, or need them only rarely.

Robes of Honour

One of the biggest Zen training temples in Japan gets quite a lot of pilgrims and has about two hundred monks in spite of the fact that it is situated in rather a remote place. They insist that pilgrims stay overnight and attend the 3.30 a.m. service which sometimes goes on for a couple of hours. Those who preside and take these great ceremonies wear magnificent gold and silver embroidered robes—masterpieces of the art.

On one occasion the head monk, whom I had come to know, was conducting the service. I was sitting in the front row of what one might call the 'resident guests'. In fine presence and making a splendid spectacle, he passed before us in this gorgeous robe, catching my eye as he went. Of course, he gave no sign of recognition.

Two or three days afterwards I was talking to him in his room. He was wearing the usual plain robe of the ordinary monk, despite his high position in the temple, and he mentioned the ceremony of the other day. He said, 'You know, those wonderful robes that I sometimes wear for the ceremonies, they're not mine. Tomorrow somebody else will be wearing them. They belong to the temple, not to me; they're just on me for the ceremony. Afterwards I take them off, deposit them, and come back into my room. And now I am myself.'

That was all he said, but he meant it as a lesson. Not only the robes in the ceremony, but the robes of honour in the world—they are not ours. They are only on us for a time. Then they have to be returned. While we are wearing them, we are not ourselves; we have to be able to take them off, deposit them, and then be ourselves.

A master who trained Tsuji Somei was a prominent roshi. He lived to be nearly a hundred, and he brushed two Chinese characters which he presented to me. They mean: *Like a fool*. Robes of honour are not appropriate to fools, but if they do happen to fall on such people and they pride themselves on them, they are worse than fools. So we should just keep *like a fool*.

This has certain advantages. To be a fool is to have no reputation, nothing to keep up, no obligations, and is in this sense an indicator for our spiritual and worldly life.

When you are wearing magnificent robes, you can't really do anything in them except look magnificent. You can't very well go gardening in full evening dress; your gleaming wing collar and shirt are quite unsuitable. In fact, evening dress is meant to separate you entirely from work or activity. This does not mean that working clothes necessarily have to be dirty or untidy; they simply ought to be appropriate. It is not wrong to put on a robe just occasionally, but if we take to wearing one all the time, it hampers us. We become tailors' dummies for the robes to hang on.

Furthermore, many so-called honours are false. For example, a man is listed in the *Guinness Book of Records* together with his photograph. He is, understandably, proud of his achievement. But when he enquires the following year whether his record still holds for a listing in the new edition, he is not only told that his record has been beaten, but that it had, in fact, been smashed by a man in New Zealand prior even to his entry last year. Unable to get all the details before going to press, the editors had used his 'second best' as a substitute. 'Of course,' the editors tell him, 'there will be an apology in the new edition, saying that the reported record last year was no record at all.'

Our moment of glory in these robes of honour is temporary, and is often a false one. Achievements in the world are of a similar nature. I knew a very good judo man in Japan in the 1930s who later became a good engineer and businessman. After the war he became a millionaire and once took me to the Millionaires Club in Tokyo. I looked round at the other millionaires and said to him, 'What is the common element between all these people?' He looked and said thoughtfully, 'Luck! I don't say some of them haven't worked very hard, or aren't very clever, but there are others who have worked just as hard and are just as clever, and who have not done so well. These people were in the right place at the right time. That's just luck! Some small success comes from work and cleverness, but the biggest element of their great success has been luck.'

We think that the success we have in life is us. The lesson of the robes, or one of them, is that it comes to us, it doesn't belong to us, and will leave us. If we hang on to robes of success, we shall not only be disappointed when they go, but we shall also not be able to do much that is useful while we are wearing them.

The aura of the robe can be false—as in the example of the *Guinness Book of Records*—but sometimes it is not so simple to decipher. When I was a student I was very keen on chess. Some of the Arab fellow students used to say that Western chess players didn't really know about chess. And the Persians used to claim that it was *their* game—the word 'check' deriving from Persian *shah*, meaning 'king', and 'checkmate' from the Persian *shah-mat*, meaning 'the king is dead'.

'You copied the whole game from us,' they used to say, 'just as you copied so many other things, such as *al-jabr* (calculation), from the Arabs.'

One day I cornered one of them and he had to play against me. I suggested tossing a coin to decide who would be White and have the first move, but he waved his hand, 'I'll take Black. All the masters prefer Black.' So I made the opening move, and I made it a cautious one. Now, he adopted a very risky policy, which contains traps for both sides—he mirrored the moves I made, so that the Black and White formations were symmetrical. One would have thought that White would have the advantage, but as a matter of fact it can be very tricky; there are some subtle traps. I felt quite nervous, not knowing all the traps, but knowing they would be there. He, meanwhile, was making his moves quickly and with confidence, still echoing mine. When I played pawn to queen's rook three, he instantly played the same move from his Black side. The position was getting more and more tense. Not knowing what to do, I moved my bishop and gave a rather futile *check*! I knew it could give no advantage; he could meet it easily by interposing. But, to my amazement, instead of interposing, he moved his own bishop and said *check*! This was against all the rules of the game. I stared at the board. One of the other Arabs who had been watching us burst out laughing. 'Fooled you there, didn't we. I told him to copy your moves for as long as he could.' I realized that this 'master' I had been playing, had no idea of chess at all. I laughed too, and we shook hands.

I was sixteen at the time, and it was quite a little lesson for the future. Sometimes, in judo, a man will come forward holding out just one hand instead of the usual two. This can mean he is either very good, or very bad. You soon find out, but to begin with you don't know. The point underlying this uncertainty is that although these robes may be either imitation or genuine, in both cases they are not the real person, and you need to find out who is.

Chess is always encouraged by tyrants. The mock Chinese saying is: *You cannot work out a difficult chess problem and at the same time plan a revolution!* So tyrants have always encouraged chess in all the schools in their dominions.

Even in the constitutional monarchy of democratic Japan, every Japanese newspaper has a sizeable chess column. Every day, there is a long commentary on the moves of the current tournament. These are big national events, and the man who for ten years won almost all of them dominated the whole field for that time. His name was Oyama, and I knew him quite well.

He had an interesting history. When he was a small boy of twelve he was fascinated by *shogi*, the Japanese form of chess—played on a bigger board than ours, with more pieces. And he wanted to be a chess master, even then. He lived in the Osaka area, so he went to the chief *dojo* (centre) in Osaka and managed to get an interview with the head teacher there, a famous master who had trained champions.

In response to his request to become an apprentice, the teacher gave him a few little tests, watched him play, and then said he could not take the boy on as a pupil as he did not have the talent. Little Oyama wept and begged and kept coming back. The teacher spoke to him seriously, 'I won't take you as a pupil and raise false hopes in you. It would not be fair to you, and it would not be fair to me and the reputation of this *dojo*. Think of something else, table tennis perhaps, in which you might do well. But you haven't got the talent for *shogi*.'

Well, the boy cried again and continued to haunt the place. Finally, the teacher said, 'I won't take you on as a pupil. But if you want, after school, you can come here and wipe the tables and help serve the tea. You can also watch the play and maybe someone will give you a game or two.' The teacher probably thought that the boy would lose his crazy idea after a year or so.

However, Oyama did not lose his commitment, and soon, as he showed extraordinary aptitude for the game, the teacher willingly enrolled him as a pupil. Ultimately, he became a star of stars, unbeaten for ten years. It is an example of a very experienced trainer ruling out as talentless a potential super-champion.

When Oyama achieved his hundredth tournament victory, there was a big celebration in his honour. I wasn't in Japan at the time, but read his acceptance speech. In it he said, 'In my career I have scored one hundred major victories, that is quite true. However, in my career I've also scored two hundred defeats. But happily we are not talking about that now, are we?' I very much admired the fact that he was not deluded by the tremendous acclamation which was showered on him. He was able to rise above it, in a humorous way.

The great Zen master, Bukko, said that if you get to the heights of anything, you are like a man who is on top of a mountain with all his possessions. When you and your things are on the top of a mountain, you have to keep hanging on to everything for dear life in order to prevent your possessions rolling down into the valley. 'It is,' he says, 'best not to be on the heights, therefore, but to be down below where you can have the things and keep them.'

When we can't wait for other people to honour us, we tend to put robes of honour on ourselves. There is one story about the great Saigo—the samurai who was absolutely free from the fear of death. He was also politically active, a prominent figure in the Meiji Restoration in Japan of 1868.

These were dangerous times in Japan and three men in Tokyo, who fanatically opposed his policies, decided to assassinate him. Not knowing where he lived, and assuming his house would be guarded, they approached a prominent Tokyo politician, Katsu Kaishu, who had once been an opponent of Saigo but who was now his friend, and with whom one of the assassins had an acquaintance. They concocted a plausible story, and asked Katsu for a letter of introduction to Saigo, which would give them the address and get them past the guard. Katsu agreed, but he had his doubts about their story. He went out to his study and came back with a sealed envelope, addressed to Saigo. He wrote his own name across the seal, and said impressively, 'Hand that in.' They took it confidently, but he had actually written to warn Saigo against them.

Unaware of this and well satisfied, they made the journey. They were slightly disconcerted to find that Saigo apparently lived still in a smallish, slightly shabby house in a far from fashionable quarter. Despite becoming a leading figure, Saigo had never moved into any sort of mansion. Moreover, he would not wear fine clothes. So when a burly man in a cheap robe came to the door in answer to their ring, they thought he must be a servant. They handed over their letter of introduction, 'This is from the noble Katsu Kaishu to the noble Saigo Takamori, to introduce us. You hand it over to him.'

To their amazement, the supposed servant said, 'I am Saigo,' and opened the letter and read: *I think the bearers of this note may be intending to kill you. Please take precautions.* Saigo looked at them, 'So you've come all the way from Tokyo to kill me, it seems,' he said conversationally, 'You must be tired after the long journey.'

A neighbour who saw the incident said that they were so taken aback by his perfect calm that they looked at each other and then left without a word. This was the sort of man he was.

He wrote some maxims for handling life. One of them is along these lines:

When a man sets about some undertaking, he generally completes seven or eight tenths of it, but rarely succeeds with the remaining two tenths This is because at the beginning a man fully restrains his egoism and respects the work itself. Results begin to come and he gets some reputation. But then egoism stirs, the prudent and restrained attitude is relaxed, pride and boasting flourish. With a confidence born of his achievements so far, he plans to complete the work for his own ends. But his efforts have become bungling, and the end is failure, all invited by himself. Therefore, restrain the self and be careful not to heed what others do or say.

In these ways, we put robes of honour on ourselves, and they hamper us and we can't do the job properly.

In judo there is a certain grading contest called 'one-against-ten.' You have to take on ten men—one after another. They are generally a couple of grades below you, and with luck half of them are so terrified of you, that it is easy to dispose of them. But one or two of them think, 'Everybody knows I'm going to lose anyway, so I've nothing to lose,' and they come shooting at you, taking fantastic risks. Because you are so sure of your own superiority, which he doesn't seem to recognize, and because he comes straight at you—'whoosh'—you can't get the robes of self-conceit and assurance off in time, so that, once in a blue moon, he scores. Then you know what it is like to look an utter fool. This has happened to some rather famous contest men who were not fully alert because they felt it was not necessary. They had already put on the robes of their coming victory. No longer simply the judo champions they ought to be, they became judo champions combined with something restricting—judo champions in cumbersome robes of honour.

In the wider sense, putting robes on ourselves infects even the best actions. I may be being philanthropic by putting a gold coin in the bowl, but if I cough while I'm doing it, then the action is infected. I'm using it partly for my own sake and partly as a generous action. I get the illusion that, somehow, if the offering is worth more, it is more generous. But that is not so at all. I have been lucky; I happen to have more money, so I put a tiny bit more money in. That is not more generous than someone who has been unlucky, has very little, and puts in only a copper.

We know this in theory, but it is extremely difficult for a wealthy man not to feel that he can buy his way into everything, including the Kingdom of Heaven. Christ said that a rich man had no more chance of getting in than a camel of getting through the eye of a needle, and in India the saying is used of an elephant.

One Indian teacher, echoing his whole tradition, used to say, 'When you find that you are becoming respected and honoured, that's the time to leave.'

Echoing this view, the Chinese recount the case of a Taoist master who had a very promising pupil. The pupil finally attained enlightenment, and the enlightened pupil became a teacher, a very famous one. Often, on the veranda outside his house, many shoes were to be seen deposited by pupils. One day his own old teacher happened to pass that way and he saw all the shoes. He waited, and when they had all gone he went in to visit his pupil. He told him, 'Get away at once! Don't hang about here a moment longer.'

Well, this is one tradition; it may not be the same in all traditions, but it is worth remembering. Do what you are to do, and then go! Don't hang about.

A chess champion in this part of the world isn't regarded as a particularly remarkable human being. He is thought of only as extremely good at chess. But in the Far East the training tries to cultivate a sort of inner balance, courage, and inspiration. Some famous masters have written best sellers on this inner training; it is not just working out chess combinations.

In Japan I was permitted to go in and watch one champion, Kimura, playing in a big tournament. They don't play championships in public; they do it in a private room. However, it is recorded on a huge board in a neighbouring hall where the public can see it and ask questions of a commentator-master. They think it is ridiculous to have hundreds of people watching two men playing chess, as we do. Is there any game with less visible action to watch than chess?

During the tournament that I sat watching, there was only one move that Kimura could make. But he didn't make it. He just sat there. I thought, 'Has he fallen asleep?' He was playing against a much younger man who had a brilliant future before him. Kimura had only one possible move. His opponent was fanning himself, drinking tea, going to the toilet, coming back and settling himself carefully on the cushion, and fidgeting generally. After about ten minutes Kimura made the move he had to make. His opponent responded in a flash. Then Kimura went into a trance again . . . And he won. He won because the young man made a blunder in his impatience to move the game on.

Afterwards, I met Kimura, and to my astonishment he was a fast talking wisecracking Tokyo cockney. I said to him, 'How is it that your chess personality is so different from your ordinary personality?'

He said, 'When I was young, I played many games against an old master who did what you saw me doing. Although sometimes there was only one move to make, he didn't make it. He would just sit there. I used to get so impatient and felt, 'Oh, anything to speed things up!' Consequently, as he played slower and slower, I was making moves quicker and quicker. I would reply instantly, and in my impatience I would make a blunder. I realized that although I was better than he was, I was always going to lose to him.'

Many of us can recognize this problem in some

form in our own lives. In the West, when chess masters are impatient—and some of them are—they are told to sit on their hands so as not to make a quick impulsive move. But this is just a makeshift solution. Kimura found something quite different. He said, 'I realized I would always lose. So next day I took out an empty chessboard and put it in front of me. Then I sat in front of it for an hour without moving. I did this for a few days. Then I sat in front of it for *two* hours without moving—no pieces on it—I just sat there. For a good time I was just seething inwardly, watching the clock. But, suddenly, in the second week, I felt a sort of calm. Now I can sit here; and now I can out-sit any of them.'

I watched Oyama, a later champion, in one of his big games. He had Black which meant that he had the opening move. In our chess we always decide what our opening move is going to be beforehand, and we make it immediately because there is a time limit. But when the timekeeper said 'Begin', Oyama simply sat, and he sat for what seemed like ten minutes. And then he played. I asked him afterwards, 'Why do you sit before there are any moves made at all?'

He told me, 'When you go to play chess, or anything else, you have an idea of how you are going to win. When I sit there, I give that up entirely; I give up those thoughts. I sit without thoughts, hopes and fears. And then I begin to feel what *he* is feeling and thinking. There's a current across the board, and if I have cleared my mind of how I'm going to attack and defend, then I begin to feel how he is—whether he's nervous, whether he's confident, whether he's energetic that day, whether he's dull that day. This I can begin to feel, and then I can adapt my game.'

Another thing he said was, 'One of the difficult things is to win a "won" game.' In *shogi* and chess, and at many times in life, you get into a position where you've got such a big advantage that you can definitely win. So why should this be difficult? *Shogi* or chess or any other such endeavour often leads up to a crisis whereby one side turns out to have the advantage, at which point it's a question of driving home that advantage. Yet, once you realize you have won the game, you are no longer that same person, putting in all the effort to win. Instead, complacency sets in as you prematurely assume the robes of honour, or place the laurels of victory on your head. Your efforts are impeded and your judgements affected. Because you are in a position of superiority, complete effort is no longer required, which tends to lower or impede what could be achieved. It is difficult to forget the coming victory and think with force, judgement and clear-sightedness. The coming victory in which we crown ourselves hampers our movement.

It can sometimes be doubted whether there is really anyone at all inside a set of magnificent ceremonial robes. All their stiff embroidery and the wonderful effect on those that see them can be at the expense of the true point of the ceremony. We may all know this, but we are often impressed by things we don't fully understand.

I had an early experience of this as a small boy. At the end of term, the clergyman-headmaster used to read in a deep voice a short chapter from the Book of Ecclesiastes of the Old Testament. The words were sonorous and they seemed to reverberate in the head. I thought, 'How wonderful! It's all in the Bible, so it must be true.' But as to what it actually meant . . ? 'When it's holy,' I thought, 'I don't suppose one can expect to understand.' This is the main part of the passage that the headmaster used to read to us at the end of every term.

> While the sun, or the light, or the moon, or the stars, be not darkened, nor the clouds return after the rain:
>
> In the day when the keepers of the house shall tremble, and the strong men shall bow themselves, and the grinders cease because they are few, and those that look out of the windows be darkened,
>
> And the doors shall be shut in the streets, when the sound of the grinding is low, and he shall rise up at the voice of the bird, and all the daughters of musick shall be brought low;
>
> Also, when they shall be afraid of that which is high, and fears shall be in the way, and the almond

tree shall flourish, and the grasshopper shall be a burden, and desire shall fail: because man goeth to his long home, and the mourners go about the streets:

Or ever the silver cord be loosed, or the golden bowl be broken, or the pitcher be broken at the fountain, or the wheel broken at the cistern;

Ecclesiastes 12, v 2-6

The mere words painted pictures: . . *the almond tree shall flourish. . .* Where? . . *he shall rise up at the voice of the bird . . .* Why? . . *the strong men shall bow themselves . . . . . the keepers of the house shall tremble . . . . . silver cord loosed . . .* What for? . . *or the golden bowl be broken . . .* Can it be? . . *pitcher . . . well . . . wheel . . . cistern . . .*

The old translation has a wonderful swing, and paints magical but disjointed pictures, with golden bowl and silver cord, and daughters of music and almond trees. But we were never told what it meant. And we never asked! Scriptures are full of passages like this. It was years later that I discovered that these are beautiful allusive descriptions of old age. *The almond tree blossom is white*: this is the white hair of age. *The keepers of the house will tremble*, means that the knees will begin to shake. *Strong men shall bow themselves*, means the back will become bent. *Those who look out of windows will be darkened*, is the failing sight. These are periphrases, surpassingly beautiful and perceptive of old age. But we didn't know. *He shall rise up at the voice of a bird*, is the people waking up very early.

Perhaps our headmaster thought some of the explanations might be embarrassing. *The clouds shall return after the rain*, is a riddle. I have heard a clergyman say he thought it meant that when you are old and you get some little ailment, you recover and think it's passed, only for it to return again. But, of course, it has a much more literal meaning than that. The words are very beautiful, wonderful, verbal robes, but they half conceal what is really meant. We have to find the deeper meaning in them.

Sengai picture of chess

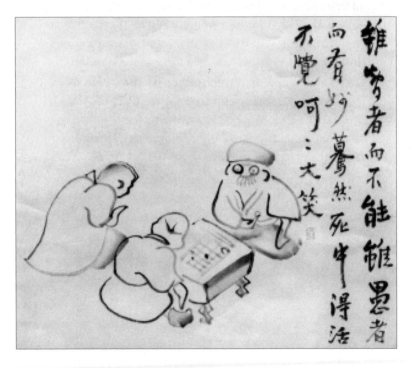

That side a learned man,
But he isn't good at chess;
This side a stupid man,
But he knows the tricks!

Even at the point of mate
He can find a way out,
Wah-ha! Unconsciously
The third man laughs.

Sengai was a famous Zen priest who presided over a large and prosperous temple, and was still more famous for his drawings, paintings and poems.

Though a master of traditional styles, his work has mostly an unconventional appearance, often with a refined humour. But underneath there is often a deep meaning for those interested in such things.

Though he lived a long life of eighty-eight years, he showed no attachment to the favours and honours showered on him by influential aristocrats and men of power; in this era when fine distinctions of rank were strictly observed, he treated all the same.

Disrobing

A new Governor of Kyoto made a call on the Abbot of the ancient temple complex of Daitokuji, on the northern outskirts of Kyoto. According to custom, he was received by an attendant monk, who then held out to him a little circular tray on which to place his visiting card. This was to be taken to the Abbot so that he would know who was the visitor, and perhaps give any directions that might be necessary. The Governor laid on his card:

Masami Takeda
Governor of Tokyo Prefecture

The attendant took the card but returned with it still on the tray, which he held out to the Governor.

The visitor stared at it for a moment and then said, 'Oh, I made a mistake.' He took out his fountain pen and put a line through the words Governor of Tokyo Prefecture. The card now just read Masami Takeda and the attendant took it back. From the next room he heard the Abbot's voice, 'Ah, Takeda. Yes, I wanted to see that fellow. Bring him in!'

The Author

Trevor Leggett is one of the leading writers on Zen Buddhism in the West today. He lived for a considerable time in Japan. He was the first foreigner to obtain the Sixth Dan (senior teachers degree) in judo from Kodokan and has written several well-known books on the subject. His other books include: *The Chapter of the Self, The Dragon Mask, Encounters in Yoga and Zen, Fingers and Moons, A First Zen Reader, Lotus Lake Dragon Pool, Realization of the Supreme Self, Sankara on the Yoga Sutras, A Second Zen Reader, Shogi: Japan's Game of Strategy, The Spirit of Budo, Three Ages of Zen, The Warrior Koans,* and *Zen and the Ways.*

Other Publications Available from BPG

Zen Teaching of Instantaneous Awakening
Master Hui Hai, Translated by John Blofeld
ISBN 0-946672-03-2

An eighth-century T'ang Dynasty text. Hui Hai was a great Zen master of the same spiritual tradition as Hui Neng, Ma Tsu and Huang Po. His direct style is as relevant today as twelve hundred years ago. 'When things happen,' says Hui Hai, 'make no response: keep your minds from dwelling on anything whatsoever: keep them for ever still as the void and utterly pure (without stain): and thereby spontaneously attain deliverance.'

Mud and Water: A Collection of Talks
Zen Master Bassui, Translated by Arthur Braverman

The only comprehensive record of the talks of this fourteenth-century Zen master. His central message was that the act of seeing one's original nature is Buddhahood itself.

Experience Beyond Thinking:
A Practical Guide to Buddhist Meditation
Diana St Ruth   ISBN 0-946672-26-1

A straightforward and easy-to-follow guide on how to begin meditating and observing what lies behind the thinking mind.

Buddhism Now

A quarterly magazine which offers a range of articles from the various Buddhist traditions.

Send £2.50 or $4 for a sample issue.